D0955290

DIMENSIONS OF PRAYER

DIMENSIONS
OF
PRAYER

Cultivating a Relationship with God

Foreword by E. Glenn Hinson

Douglas V. Steere

UPPER
ROOM BOOKS
NASHVILLE

Published in the United States by Upper Room Books

Originally published by the Women's Division,
General Board of Global Ministries, The United Methodist Church

Cover art direction: Michele Wetherbee
Cover design: Stefan Gutemuth
Interior design: Steve Diggs & Friends

The Upper Room Web Site: http://www.upperroom.org

First printing: May 1997

Library of Congress Cataloging-in-Publication Data
Steere, Douglas Van, 1901–
Dimensions of prayer : cultivating a relationship with God /
Douglas V. Steere : foreword by E. Glenn Hinson.
p.   cm.
Includes bibliographical references.
ISBN 0-8358-0800-9 (hc)
1. Prayer.   I.Title.
BV210.2.S7   1996
248.3′2—dc20   96-43268
CIP

Printed in the United States of America

To

Bess Crandell

whose life has been a channel of encouragement

CONTENTS

Foreword   xi

Introduction   xv

CHAPTER 1 ——————————————— 1

Prayer and the Human Situation

Creatureliness and Prayer

A Redeeming Order Is Already at Work

The Game of Hide-and-Seek

''God Not on the Borders of Life but at Its Center''

What Do We Do When We Pray?

Devotional Reading and Prayer

Prayer and Autosuggestion

Prayer and Meditation

Prayer as a Response to Divine Encompassment

Spoken Prayers and Attention

Silent Prayer and Waiting on God

Dealing with Distractions in Prayer

CHAPTER 2 ——————————————— 32

To Pray Is to Change

To Come Near to God Is to Change

Prayer and the Chamber of Loving Scrutiny

Prayer and the Cost of Renewal

Why Do We Stop Our Prayers?

On Accepting the Forgiveness of God

Prayer and Adoration

Some Positive Side Effects of Adoration

CHAPTER 3 ———————————————————— 51

The Power of Prayer

On Authentic Asking in Prayer

Beginning Where You Are

On Having "Far Too Much Sense for Everything We Do"

Does Prayer Change Things?

Prayer and the Divine Strategy

Prayer and the "Laws of Nature"

The Social Dimension in Prayer: Intercession

Intercession and the Continuous Siege of Souls

"When I Pray, Coincidences Happen"

The Cost of Intercessory Prayer

Prayer and Spiritual Healing

CHAPTER 4 ———————————————————— 80

The Dialogue of Prayer and Action

The Seeds of Concern

Concerns and Rational Scrutiny

Foreign and Domestic Mutations

"A Man on the Cross Sends Me Back Again"

Christian Prayer and Ethical Intensification

What of Prayer without Ceasing?

Prayer and the "Night Shifts"

Private Prayer and Corporate Worship

"Lent to Be Spent"

Notes   103

FOREWORD

Douglas Steere (1901–1995) spent most of his life getting to know God and teaching others how to know God. Early in an eventful and profoundly meaningful life he discovered the centrality and significance of attentiveness to "that love which is at the heart of things." As a graduate student at Harvard during a time when he questioned "the worth of going on living," an Oxford Group Movement meeting marked "a turning point" in his life as he turned inward for strength. Again, as he prepared to take the comprehensive examinations for admission to the Ph.D. in philosophy, a half hour on his knees pulled him past the wobbly stage and confirmed the rightness of going on, taking the exams quietly, and accepting the consequences for what he had written. As a Rhodes scholar at Oxford, he "experienced a deep and moving corporate Quaker silence" and felt drawn also to the Roman Catholic Church "with all of its inviting buildings open for prayer throughout the day."

Employment in a Quaker college as a colleague of Quaker leader Rufus Jones tilted the scales toward the Friends, and he had profoundly moving experiences in the meetings of these Protestant contemplatives. One occurred in Stockholm as he led in organizing the Quaker Finnish Relief effort in July 1945 at the end of World War II: "About 8:50 I gave a brief prayer that came of itself and then Fred [Tritten] prayed," he reported in a letter to Dorothy Steere, "and in a flash I was melted down and the glorious release of the life of God was mine for an instant. My face was wet with tears and I felt that nothing in the world mattered that could disturb this certainty, and I felt ever so close to each one there and as we closed I saw two others who seemed to be having the same moving experience."

Profound as was his debt to the Friends, however, Douglas Steere did not confine his gleanings about prayer to them. He drew insights from everywhere in the vast treasury of Christianity and Judaism and even other world religions. From his study of Baron von Hügel in the 1920s and the time when, in 1933, he took a one-month retreat in the famous Benedictine monastery at Maria Laach in Germany, he did not stop sponging up wisdom of the great masters of prayer—the psalmists, Jesus, the desert fathers and mothers, Benedict of Nursia, Bernard of Clairvaux, Hildegard of Bingen, Teresa of Ávila, Isaac Penington, John Woolman, Amelia Fogelklou Norlind, Thomas Kelly, Dorothy Day, and Thomas Merton.

Although a member of a religious group numbering only about 200,000 worldwide, Douglas Steere was an ecumenical pioneer. He represented the Society of Friends as an official Observer Delegate in three of the four sessions of the Second Vatican Council and participated in the Lambeth Quadriennial of the Church of England in 1968. In 1967, while serving as Chairman of the Friends World Committee for Consultation, he organized dialogues between Christians and Buddhists in Japan and Christians and Hindus in India. An exceptional speaker, he lectured in colleges, universities, and seminaries all over the world and wrote books and essays by invitation from numerous other religious bodies.

Douglas Steere distilled much of his profound experience and vast learning and poured them into this beautiful book. He has helped us to answer those perplexing but utterly essential questions we often fear to voice: Why we pray, what prayer is, how to pray, and what prayer does to us and to our activity in the world. This is a book for beginners, which all of us are when it comes to knowing God, but it is one that will nurture those who have searched all their lives.

E. Glenn Hinson
Professor of Spirituality and John Loftis Professor of
   Church History
Baptist Theological Seminary at Richmond

INTRODUCTION

"Be still before the Lord, and wait patiently for him" (Psalm 37:7, RSV). What a strangely alien prescription the psalmist gives here for the fiercely active life of our time. We live in a culture that is not used to stillness; we are not schooled either in waiting or in patience. It has been suggested that in our time we are not suffering as much from a decay of beliefs as from a loss of solitude. With the loss of solitude has come an inner alienation: "We are cut off outside ourselves."

Charles Williams opens his striking novel *All Hallows Eve*[1] with an account of two souls who are hovering over a city where a car accident has just taken their lives. They cannot return to earth and yet they do not feel able to leave it. They are confused, not knowing who they are or why they have lived. They are not only confused about themselves, but are also numb and oblivious to the human needs that surround them. They seem perilously close to the condition that George Bernanos described when he declared, "Hell is not to love any more."[2] They were not ready to die. They, like we all, were meaning to take some time out for stillness and quietude someday, but they had indefinitely postponed it, and now they are adrift.

If we were to take waiting and patience seriously, we would soon discover that these attitudes were not prescribed for themselves alone. Implicit in the psalmist's encouragement of their use is his knowledge that waiting and patience are postures of receptivity.

If something apart from ourselves is seeking to make itself known to us, it will not succeed unless we know how to wait, and to persist in waiting. In this recommendation of the psalmist—to wait and to be patient—there may be a hint that there is more than one way to prepare ourselves to receive this self-disclosing Reality. There may even be an intimation that science, with its aggressive and relentless methods of investigating the physical and biological skim of the world, has not necessarily given us the best method for opening ourselves to that in which the skim is grounded.

There is a claim here that stillness, waiting, and patience before the Lord are authentic dimensions of human perception. These dimensions have been scandalously undervalued and ignored in our time. They need to be reinstated and used with an intensity of dedication comparable to that found in the pursuits of scientific investigation. It is the purpose of this little book to encourage precisely such practice and dedication, believing that "prayer is for the religious life what original research is for science."

In trying, as Søren Kierkegaard says, "to become a Christian . . . when one is a Christian of a sort,"[3] there is no instrument that is so directly designed to this purpose as the practice of private prayer. "I am convinced that the gate by which we enter the castle is prayer and meditation,"[4] insists Teresa of Ávila, that wise and masterly sixteenth-century guide in prayer. "Prayer is the mortar that holds our house together."[5]

The assumption of this book will be that those who read it are not looking for a book of Christian apologetics but for a workbook on prayer. It is addressed to those who are already within the Christian community and who are there, not for a brief stay, as at a vacation resort, but for what they expect to be a permanent residence. There is an old story of an Arab and an Englishman who proposed to race their horses against each other. All went well until the length of the race was being agreed upon. The Englishman proposed a race of an hour, but the Arab would listen to nothing less than three days, insisting that an hour's race would reveal nothing whatever of the stamina of a horse! In a striking way enduring faithfulness in prayer reveals the stamina of the Christian.

On the other hand, preacher and writer P. T. Forsyth has scathing words for long-term religious people for whom the Christian life is not a school of constant inward growth: "How is it that the experience of life is so often barren of spiritual culture for religious people? They become stoic and stalwart, but not humble; they have keen sight, but no insight. . . . At sixty they are, spiritually, much where they were at twenty-six."[6] The condition that he describes and that we know all too well in ourselves and in our associates is like that of a visitor to an embryological museum who is unable to get beyond contemplating the jar containing the two-month embryo.

In the long pull of yielding ourselves to God, of coming under the guidance of the inward Christ, there can be no standing still. The religion of Jesus Christ is not a holding operation. In the flyleaf of English leader Oliver Cromwell's Bible was penned, "He that is not getting better is getting worse." What we secretly long for is to *grow* into the men and women that God in his infinite yearning means us to become. We are not content, like a local car-ferry, to hug the shallows and to shuttle safely back and forth across a comfortably narrow strait. We secretly long for God's seaway, and we have hints that God is calling us into real discipleship and that, in our prayerlessness, we are not responding.

We know what the French Quaker Marius Grout meant when he wrote, "I believe in the influence of silent and radiant [people] and I say to myself that such [people] are rare. They, nevertheless, give savor to the world. . . . Nothing will be lost here so long as such [people] continue to exist. If there is a wish we should make today, it is that we might see in ourselves the beginnings of contemplation."[7]

In religious circles we find today a fierce and almost vio-

lent planning and programming, a sense that without ceaseless activity nothing will ever be accomplished. How seldom
it occurs to us that God has to undo and to do all over again
so much of what we in our willfulness have pushed through
in God's name. How little there is in us of the silent and
radiant strength in which the secret works of God really take
place! How ready we are to speak, how loath to listen, to
sense the further dimension of what it is that we confront.

In fourteenth-century England there were holy women
who settled each in a little room at the base of some church
and gave themselves to a life of prayer, especially prayer for
the church and its members. These women were called by
the quaint but telling name of anchoress; they were indeed
spiritual anchors in that they held the church amid the
storms of that century. Could it be that there is some way of
translating this medieval passion for self-dedication and the
practice of prayer into the idiom of our time? Could not the
same spiritual firming up and renewal of the church today
be carried on from within by men and women whose lives of
prayer are placed freely at God's disposal?

Devotion of a life to prayer and contemplation—*this* is not
the passivity of spirit some call quietism. Marius Grout is
right in saying, "If contemplation, which introduces us to
the very heart of creation, does not inflame us with such
love that it gives us, together with deep joy, the understand-

ing of the infinite misery of the world, it is a vain kind of contemplation, it is the contemplation of the face of a false God. The sign of true contemplation is charity. By your capacity for forgiveness shall I recognize your God and also by your opening your arms to all creation."[8]

There is no attempt in this book to describe the invaluable assistance that those who embark on prayer can get from prayer fellowship groups. We need desperately the company of honest companions on this road. Nor is there any description here of the use, once or twice a year, of the two- or three-day retreats where, in a house apart and under the direction of an experienced retreat guide, a group of people are taken into a "school of prayer"—which is precisely what every retreat should be. There is also no discussion here of specific books of devotional literature, although helpful guides to the classics abound. The Upper Room, for example, has issued a series of convenient pocket books of selected devotional classics that can be warmly recommended for use.

In learning to pray, no laboratory is needed but a room, no apparatus but ourselves. The living God is the field of force into which we enter in prayer, and the only really fatal failure is to stop praying and not to begin again.

I would like to offer special thanks to Anna Petit Broomell for her immensely helpful scrutiny of the manuscript for style, to Mildred Hargreaves for her admirable typing of the manuscript, and to my wife for assistance at every point.

Douglas V. Steere
Haverford, Pennsylvania

CHAPTER ONE

PRAYER *and the* HUMAN SITUATION

There is much to be said for an approach to prayer that proceeds in proper order. Once C. C. J. Webb, a distinguished Christian philosopher, told me of how scrupulous he was about this matter of order when he presented his prestigious Gifford Lectures on "God and Personality." The first set of ten lectures was not on humankind's personal dimensions or even on the human soul at prayer. It was on God. Only then was he ready to turn to the second set on human personality.

Certainly men and women come to prayer out of many different necessities, and they use a hundred human-made ladders in their efforts to get the first handholds. Yet causes and means may all be quite incidental. Too early a focus upon practical *methods* of prayer may lead only to confusion as to which plan to follow. At the outset, it is important for us to note that, back of the human condition, and accounting for it, is the Ground, the One whom humankind confronts: *God*. Any sound treatment of prayer must put first things first and begin with God. Unless there is a God of whom we can say with Ignatius of Loyola, "I come from God, I belong to God, I return to God," prayer is a mockery. We pause, therefore, at the beginning of this handbook to give a swift look at the cosmic setting in which Christian prayer is placed.

CREATURELINESS *and* PRAYER

I come from God: Implicit in this assertion, which is the ground—foundation, basis—of all Christian prayer, is an acknowledgment of my dependence upon God. But it does not stop at a confession of my personal dependence upon God. We are bold enough, even in an age of science like our own, to go on to acknowledge the ultimate dependence of the complex processes of nature, of which I am a minute part, upon God as their source and conserver. In doing so, we are not brashly claiming to have fully plumbed the depths of the mystery of nature. But neither must we relinquish the claim made in the writings of Paul (Ephesians 1:9–10) and John (John 1:1–5) that a divine plan is being worked out in the whole cosmos. The person who prays may have no airtight philosophical arguments on hand to help him or her to prove for once and for all this faith. He or she does, however, believe that a Guarantor exists who accounts for the intelligibility of nature—an intelligibility on which the very possibility of scientific inquiry depends.

Augustine, in a classic passage in the tenth book of the *Confessions,* gives something of the flavor of a person of prayer approaching nature. The mystery remains, but so does the inward conviction that this is my Father's world. "What is the object of my love?" Augustine asked.

> I asked the earth and it said: "It is not I." I asked all that is in it; they made the same confession (Job 28:12f.). I asked the sea, the deeps, the living creatures that creep, and they responded: "We are not your God, look beyond us." I asked the breezes which blow and the entire air with its inhabitants . . . heaven, sun, moon and stars; they said: "Nor are we the God whom you seek." And I said to all these things in my external environment: "Tell me of my God who you are not, tell me something about him." And with a great voice they cried out: "He made us" (Ps. 99:3). . . . "We are not God" and "He made us."[1]

Henry T. Hodgkin used to insist that people could never move into a spiritual relation to the universe and its Source until they acknowledge their dependence. He put it in terms of host and guest, suggesting that the person who plays host in the universe, and regards God as the guest, can never really pray. Only when the transmutation occurs and we discover that in this universe not we but God serves as the host, and not God but we are the guests—and highly transitory guests—is prayer really possible. When that takes place what spiritual writer Baron von Hügel so happily called a sense of *creatureliness* wells up in the mind and heart. Creatureliness is the mark in a person of the acknowledgment, either implicit or explicit, that "We are not God and He made us." When this acknowledgment comes, prayer is natural to us.

The importance of nature, then, cannot be ignored or overlooked in any full-bodied life of prayer. It has its abyss of mystery that quickens humankind to wonder. It has its semiconscious "otherness" that science explores and that the person of religion, to his or her infinite profit, is compelled to confront. There is an astringent quality in this otherness that purges and cleanses the religious person of any inclination for self-absorption, for seeing God as too small. It braces him or her to find not only a God of personal dimensions but a God of the cosmos—the orderly universe—in which the personal drama is laid. (See Psalm 8:3–4.)

A REDEEMING ORDER IS ALREADY *at* WORK

I belong to God: We do not project or generate grace. Nor do we initiate the redemptive order or process which, when we let it, sweeps into its course our scarred lives, our prayers, and our concerns for others. The redemptive process is already going on. It sprang out of the heart of the Creator of nature; it is a kind of second creation. It is directed to free souls who, in spite of belonging to God and owing all to God, are yet free to reject and repulse God's costly advances. There is a company of the redeemed, a communion of faithful souls, both living and dead, who join with Christ and the Father in laying siege to the heart of the world. The cross is the symbol of the costly caring of this second creation, of this redemptive love. Philosopher/theologian Blaise Pascal, having in mind this inward siege of the heart of every person who lives, declares in his *Thoughts,* "Jesus will be in agony even to the end of the world."[2]

When Nicholas of Cusa, the fifteenth-century spiritual guide, sent along the manuscript of his *The Gaze of God* to the group for whom he had written it, he accompanied it by a painting of the all-seeing eye of God, which was to be hung in the chapel during the reading of the manuscript. There may be wisdom in following this example of the medieval use of visual aids. Let us seek, at this point, then, to hang in the gallery of our minds not one, but several, pictures that will illustrate the costly business of God's redemption, and present afresh this claim that *"I belong to God."*

A picture that hung in many a Christian home decades ago depicted Jesus as a shepherd. His feet were braced; one hand closed over the branch of a tree, and he was perilously leaning over a deep cleft while with his free hand he was seizing a sheep that was caught in the brambles. God's redemptive love may be seen as something like that. If the sheep waited to deserve such treatment, it would wait forever. The Abbé de Tourville in his telling *Letters* counsels, "Do not keep accounts with our Lord. . . . Go bankrupt! Let our Lord love you without justice! Say frankly, 'He loves me because I do not deserve it; that is the wonderful thing about Him; and that is why I, in my turn, love Him as well as I can without worrying. . . . I know no other way of loving God. Therefore, burn your account books!' "[3]

In the strait between the upper and lower peninsulas of Michigan, an ore boat was struck in a collision and sank. Several years later a salvage vessel was sent to raise this sunken ship. The salvage steamer had a huge prow and forward structure, and after a diver had gone down and fastened cables under the sunken ship, water was pumped into the prow of the salvage vessel until it was brought down almost to the level of the water. The cables binding it to the sunken ship were made very tight. Then the water in the salvage ship's hull was slowly pumped out so that her buoyancy lifted the sunken ship and made it possible for the salvage boat to steam a few hundred yards toward shore until her load struck bottom again. This process was repeated time after time until finally the sunken ship was so near the top of the water that air chambers could be put alongside to hold it up and float it away. Slowly, not all at once, but relentlessly involving itself, this salvage vessel carried through its rescue operations. At no less cost than allowing itself to be buried repeatedly in water over its sunken hull could the salvage ship lift its prize to the surface. God in Christ could do no less.

The Abbé Huvelin once commented to Baron von Hügel on the redemptive power of suffering and on the supreme love it exhibited. "Our Lord," he wrote, "laid hold of the world, not by fine speeches, or by the Sermon on the Mount, but by His blood, His sufferings on the cross."[4] A medieval painter once portrayed Jesus on the cross as though he had disengaged one arm and was reaching down with it to lift up to himself a petitioning follower—a person who might depict us all.

Of the story of the prodigal son, which might well have been named "A Father's Redemptive Love," someone once noted that "God came all the way down stairs" in his caring, and that at no less price could the son's heart have been touched to the quick. The redemptive process is truly depicted in these pictures and stories. The incarnate God neither slumbers nor sleeps. The heart of the gospel message is that God costingly and unceasingly cares.

THE GAME of HIDE-AND-SEEK

Each of these instances illustrates a situation in which something or someone present needs to be redeemed, restored, renewed. There is also present That which wills to redeem, restore, or renew at great cost to Itself. And the redemptive process in all its mystery is not only the revelation of costliness but also of constancy—even when spurned, even when ignored. "He was in the world . . . yet the world knew him not" (John 1:10).

There is a Jewish Hasidic story of a rabbi's son who came in drenched with tears from a game of hide-and-seek with some neighborhood playmates. When his father asked him what was the matter, his son told him that he had hidden as was expected but that no one had bothered to seek him. The rabbi drew his son to himself and tenderly told him that now, perhaps, he could for the first time know how the dear Lord felt who also hid himself in order to be sought, and who was still waiting in vain for people to seek him.

The late Oxford scholar L. P. Jacks enjoyed telling of a parlor game that he often got his guests at Shotover Hill to play. It consisted of one of the company's going for a set period into a lighted room and then, upon returning, making an inventory from memory of all that he or she had seen there. Dr. Jacks noted that almost never did a guest in his or her busy inventorying make any mention of the light by which all of the objects listed were made visible. It is equally possible for humankind, in its freedom, to overlook the operation of redemptive love.

Is there no way to get people to expand the inventory—to

coerce them to return to the seeking? Not if God is the God Christians have conceived; for, as the second-century *Epistle to Diognetus* declared, "Coercion is not an attribute of God." God, unless we are abysmally mistaken, has no place among the redeemed for conscripts. The redemptive process, into which he would draw us, is only for thankful-hearted volunteers. Yet God who besieges us with love "will neither slumber nor sleep" (Psalm 121:4), and we can never begin to understand what prayer really is unless we see it as a response to the prior initiative of God, as a response to the siege of our souls by this great redemptive company at whose center and core the yearning heart of God in the caring Christ is to be found. *I belong to God.*

"GOD NOT *on the* BORDERS *of* LIFE *but at* ITS CENTER"

I return to God: At my death, I return to the One from whom I came and to whom I belong. For regardless of how self-sufficient I, with my talents and my possessions, have assumed myself to be, when my body fails, there is then only One who can translate me into another life.

My return to God need not be postponed, however, to such an inevitable extremity. Dietrich Bonhoeffer, writing from his Nazi prison on the thirtieth of April and the twenty-fifth of May 1944, declared, "I should like to speak of God not on the borders of life but at its centre, not in weakness but in strength, not, therefore in [humankind's] suffering and death, but in . . . life and goodness. . . . God is beyond in the midst of our life. . . . We must not wait until we are at the end of our tether: [God] must be found at the centre of life: in life and not only in death . . . in activity, and not only in sin."[5]

I return to God: The fulfillment of Dietrich Bonhoeffer's longing to find God at the center of life is precisely what the Christian experience testifies to. Christ is not only *for* us—as described in the classical evangelical witness of his costly redemptive activity—Christ is also *in* us. The renewing, quickening, guiding, healing, individuating* action of God, witnessed to in the lives of those who are thus inwardly involved, gives overwhelming confirmation to Swedish Lutheran archbishop Nathan Söderblom's dying witness: "Now is eternity." God is here and now continuously revealing God's self in the souls of men and women. "Do you not feel yourself drawn with the expectation and desire of some Great Thing?" writes seventeenth-century poet and mystic Thomas Traherne. There is then "not only the contemplation of His love in the work of redemption, tho' that is wonder-

---

* EDITOR'S NOTE. *Individuating:* Being made a whole, complete individual by an inner integration of the conscious and unconscious mind that produces a transformed individual, rightly related to oneself, to God, and to one's fellow human beings.

ful, but the end for which we are redeemed; a communion with Him."[6] This end is what real prayer brings about, here and now.

It was in the very thick of life that George Fox could declare that he saw "that there was an ocean of darkness and death, but an infinite ocean of light and love, which flowed over the ocean of darkness"[7]; or that Dame Juliana of Norwich could sing in her triple refrain, "but all shall be well, and all shall be well, and all manner of thing shall be well."[8]

It was in the midst of life that Charles Andrews in India could feel inwardly drawn and quickened to pack his movable belongings into a small sack and set out on a ten-thousand-mile journey to the Caribbean to speak there for the depressed Indians, who were being shamelessly exploited by Andrews's own countrymen and -women. It is in witness to this availability of the guidance of the Christ within that Quaker Isaac Penington could declare, "There is that near you which will guide you; O wait for it, and be sure to keep to it." It is in the center of life, too, that we find John Wesley's stream of healings[9] or Quaker George Fox's classic description of a woman's recovery from an illness: "The Lord settled her mind, and she mended."

It is here, where we live our daily lives, that Søren Kierkegaard could sing out his praise to God for individuating him, "Through the unspeakable grace and help of God I have become myself."[10] Paul Claudel, a poet and statesman, could thus write his famous letter to Jacques Riviere to assure him that if he entered this stream of power, he would not likely find that his life would come to some static halt:

> One sentence in your letter made me laugh. It was when you told me you feared that in religion you might find an end to your quest—an end to strife. Dear friend, the day you receive God, you will have a guest within you who will never leave you repose. "I have not come to bring peace but a sword." On that day you will know the ferment no earthly vessel can contain, the true strife against passion and spiritual darkness, the real battle—not that in which a [person] falls, but that from which he [or she] emerges a victor.[11]

I return to God: To live the life of prayer means to emerge from my drowse, to awaken to the communing, guiding, healing, clarifying, and transforming current of God's Holy Spirit in which I am immersed. But to awaken is not necessarily to return. Awareness, no matter how vivid, must be accompanied by "a longing aye to dwell within the beauty of his countenance," and until prayer knows and is the expression of this longing, it is still callow and is likely to melt away at the first sharp thaw.

What Do We Do When We Pray?

Now, having dealt in the proper order with what we confront in prayer, with what is already going on, the elemental question is still before us: "What do we do when we pray?"

Although it may shock some pious souls, it ought to be bluntly said at the outset that the scaffolding of prayer is a human matter, that there are some plain rules of spiritual hygiene concerning it, and that they can be clearly stated.

The first of these rules is that, in order to pray, you have to stop being "too elsewhere" and to *be there*. This does not mean that you have to be in a given room, at a given time, in a given posture. It does mean that you have to care enough about this placing of yourself in an act of absolute receptivity to the Divine that what is at the heart of things may take possession of you, mind, heart, and will. You have to care enough so that you will collect yourself, move back into your own soul from the distant suburbs where much of life tends to be spent, and honestly *be there*. Robert Frost writes, "It is we ourselves who are not always there." In prayer it is a matter of being present where we are.

The author George Moore, in replying to a question of a young woman on how to go about the business of becoming a writer, suggested to her that she buy a table and a chair, get a pad of paper and a pen, and then *be there*. When the muse comes to dine with you, you have to be at home. Being present is a first condition of hospitality. But unless you want terribly to write, you will not be at the table. A thousand legitimate reasons will appear that will call you elsewhere, and anyone who has ever written knows how insistent these calls away from home, these calls from the table, can be. So it is with prayer.

The first rule in prayer, then, is that you have to *want* mightily to pray and that if that want is mighty enough, you will be present, really present, where you are. It helps to have a place, the same place, to which you go each day. It helps to have a regular time when you will appear to await the Host who may visit at your table. It helps to have a posture, whether kneeling or standing or sitting or pros-trate—or a variation of these—in which you gather your physical frame for this act of prayer. It helps to read briefly in the Bible or in some devotional classic as a warm-up. All of this is self-evident. But there are those who live where there is no privacy, those who travel a good deal, and those who have many demands made upon them by a growing family or the care of ailing elders. For them ideal conditions for prayer are simply absent. They, nevertheless, can be present wherever they are. Over a dishpan, darning socks, holding the baby, or in a monotonous work routine, they are *present where they are* and are waiting for the Host's ar-rival.

I remember an overworked missionary nurse in a hospital in Angola who told a group of us how she had complained to her superior that after her twelve hours on duty with many extra calls beyond her routine tasks, she was simply too exhausted to pray, and that her interior life had ebbed away. She had gone on to explain with special bitterness the situation with which she was faced at that moment. At the close of the day, she still had twelve more patients to wash before going off duty. After that, all she would be able to do would be to throw herself on her bed in exhaustion when she came to her room. Her older colleague heard the outburst, in love, and suggested that it was not really necessary to wait until she got home to pray. If she washed each of these next twelve as though each were the body of Christ, her praying could begin at once.

Is it not obvious that those whose table is set in the midst of activity can, if they really desire, exercise ingenuity in finding snatches of time exclusively for prayer? They will not pretend to be Brother Lawrences, the Brother Lawrences that so many of the sugary devotional treatises of our day tend to encourage. They will not entirely overlook the first ten years of faithful prayer with their desolation that Brother Lawrence spent before coming to the condition of extraordinary abundance where all of life was prayer.

I met a station attendant in mid-India who supported his entire family on thirty dollars a month. He told me how he worked until past midnight each day, rose at eight, encouraged the children to play out-of-doors, and at 8:30 found time for taking his place at the Host's table. There are few homemakers who—like the Irish woman tenement dweller whose utterly unself-conscious praying left such an indelible impression on Catholic Worker Movement founder Dorothy Day—cannot find a few moments in the morning to spend on their knees. I know a couple in favored circumstances who walk in silence for half an hour at the beginning of each morning. Some churches are open in the middle of the day for any part of the workers' noon period that can be offered, and there are, for many, the midnight watches when we share God's insomnia and come to the table that is spread and waiting.

Being present where we are has only incidentally to do with time and place and posture. Each of us will know his or her weakness and not indulge in evasion or pretense but, within the limits of the means at his or her command, will provide the opportunity needed for communication with God.

John Wesley once wrote, "Whether you like it or no, read and pray daily. It is for your life; there is no other way: else you will be a trifler all your days. . . . Do justice to your own soul; give it time and means to grow. Do not starve yourself any longer."[12]

DEVOTIONAL READING *and* PRAYER

The rule concerning devotional reading as a way of entry into prayer is not difficult to state. Teresa of Ávila wrote, "It is very helpful to read a book of devotion . . . so as to learn how to collect the thoughts, and to pray well vocally, thus, little by little, enticing the soul by coaxing and persuasion, so that it may not take alarm. . . . For more than fourteen years I could not meditate without a book."[13]

Here Teresa is describing the transition from the ordinary activities of the mind to the centered activity of prayer and is testifying that a warm-up period of reading may open the shy reaches of the deeper self in us so that effective prayer becomes more possible. We need not hesitate to make the most of such reading.

Two footnotes might be added here. There are radically different frames of mind in which the reading of a book may be approached. The use of a devotional book as a preparation for prayer would seem to call less for the sharply analytical, prosecuting-attorney stance of the mind than for a mind receptively open, not only to the truth present, but also to the truth as it relates to one's own life. Such a savoring of the reading would likely open the way for this pondering to pass readily into prayer.

A second note is important: Reading should not take the place of praying. If it precedes prayer, it should be brief, and should be broken off when one comes to a passage that makes a good gate into prayer. The temptation to substitute reading for prayer is very great, and if we succumb to it, devotional reading may become both an evasion and a temptation. We are not interested in a secondhand or vicarious spirituality.

PRAYER *and* AUTOSUGGESTION

A third rule in prayer is this: Do not be troubled by the fact that the initial stages of prayer are voluntary acts of your own surface mind. They are quite consciously devised for the purpose of focusing your attention on your relationship to God and God's redeeming love. Some persons are troubled by the feeling that prayer is nothing but autosuggestion. The only serious objection to this scruple has to do with the "nothing but."

The preliminary levels of prayer are indeed self-suggested and admittedly so. But this does not dismiss them as simply falsifiers or deceivers. The greatest evidence of humankind's freedom lies in its power to focus attention on what it chooses. In other words, we need not be the victims or the slaves of heterosuggestion, simply reacting to every random stimulus that strikes us; but we may *of our own volition* choose the direction of our attention. This power to direct attention is auto- or self-suggestion.

The fact that we are able to do this, to freely focus our attention upon what God is and is doing and on how we are related to God, does not pretend in itself to establish the truth of God's existence. The truth of God's existence must be established, if it can be established at all, by other means and by later confirmations. But it should be equally clear that because, in prayer, we have used our human power of attention in this way, focusing it on God, we have not necessarily tainted what may result from this concentration with an exclusive subjectivity or with inevitable self-deception. We have simply set the stage for the possibility of communication in the only way a human being can. We are then ready to receive those confirmations, those ranges of experience to which at least millions have testified, which take us beyond this "nothing but" level of our voluntary acts into the involuntary range of experience. There we discover what Gerhard Tersteegen meant when he wrote, "Oh what a difference when, after reason has carved an image of God, the Lord Himself comes."[14]

Then we discover what it is not only to pray, but to be prayed in and prayed through.

There are levels of prayer not discussed in this little book where the involuntary phase is the distinguishing characteristic, where little or nothing is done to induce it, and yet all is done inwardly to renew the will and make it cherish God as never before. Such prayer is simply a gift and can only be acknowledged.

The preliminary levels of prayer (discussed above, in connection with the issue of autosuggestion) are *voluntary* acts of the mind and are thus not exempt from error but must be continually tested. But if we frankly admit that deliberate or voluntary subjective acts play a considerable part in all ordinary prayer, we shall be all the more eager to make these preliminary steps of prayer as carefully as possible. We can also rid ourselves once and for all of the scruple that prayer is only a human projection.

PRAYER *and* MEDITATION

A final rule of prayer deals with what is called meditation. Meditation can be defined in different ways, but in the religious sense it customarily means thinking and pondering—in the presence of God—upon the specific meaning for us of some words we have read or some thought we have had.

The subjects for meditation may include a verse in the Bible, a line of prayer, a luminous insight that we have jotted down from our reading, or something that has happened to us. We choose our subject for meditation, focus the mind upon it, bringing the attention back again and again in order to look at the various facets of the subject, and ask ourselves not only "What does it mean?" but "What does it mean for *me?* What has it to do with *my* life?"

Now it is readily apparent that all prayer contains elements of meditation: the focusing of the wandering mind, the use of the memory and imagination, the pondering, the openness to be taught and to be shown the personal implications of what is before the one who prays. But it is also clear that there could be meditation quite apart from the deeper ranges of prayer; in fact, much general meditation might exclude these deeper ranges of prayer entirely.

This phase of prayer, therefore, conceives of meditation as an element of the preliminary levels of all prayer. Meditation resembles devotional reading in being simply a vestibule, a useful preparation, for prayer. But preliminary meditation must never be thought of as replacing prayer. For *real prayer is focused upon God and God's redemptive love* and ordinary meditation may or may not be. Real prayer is capable of rising to another level—of being drawn beyond the matters with which preliminary meditation is ordinarily concerned. But prayer and meditation can never be fully disentangled. The gentle drawing of the mind over the areas of concern in the lower levels of prayer is often quite indistinguishable from the consideration of the different facets of a subject, which is the characteristic of general meditation.

PRAYER *as a* RESPONSE *to* DIVINE ENCOMPASSMENT

Von Hügel once wrote of his own young manhood, "Certainly for myself, I know very well that when my adolescence came, it was . . . the successful awakening in me to the fact of deep reality, encompassing me on every side, that saved me."[15] With little change, this could stand for the first stage of prayer. For in prayer, our first step is to remember, to be successfully awakened to the fact of deep reality encompassing us on every side, and to want to be drawn within its range of radiation. Prayer aims at both a recognition of, and a human response to, something of cosmic significance that is already going on in the universe. François de Sales expressed this very simply by telling those who would pray to begin by remembering into Whose Presence they were to come. And Francis of Assisi used the device of repeating over and over to himself at spaced intervals, "O my God, Who art Thou? and Who am I?"

There is no hurry, however, about plunging into prayer. We may well linger in the portico to be awakened, to remember into Whose Presence we are about to come. If one of us were to be ushered into the presence of one of the great spirits of our century—Albert Schweitzer, Alan Paton, or Mother Teresa—we should be glad for a little time in the portico to collect ourselves, to adjust not our clothing, but our spirits, for meeting this one whose reputation we cherish. During this waiting period, we might well think of how this person had lived, of how he or she had spared nothing to give of self to some great human cause, and of how drawn we were to have the blessing of conversing with such a person. If this time of recollection is precious preceding a

visit to a human being, how much more suitable and necessary it is before coming into the presence of God.

SPOKEN PRAYERS *and* ATTENTION

But when we have remembered God, into whose presence
we come in prayer, how do we begin to pray? Should we use
spoken, standardized prayers or silent, spontaneous prayers?
But a prior question levels the sharpness of separation between these two forms of prayer. This prior question is one
of intent, of *attention* in prayer.

We may not be willing to go so far as spiritual writer
Simone Weil who insists that "absolute attention is prayer."
Yet this bold and unqualified statement sheaths a deep insight. If there is a longing, an intent to come under the Gaze
of God, to open the heart to God's scrutiny, to go over our
lives and their plans and relationships in God's presence; if
we feel the wave of gratitude sweeping over us at God's
being what God is—then our spoken prayer lifts us to the
Presence of God as readily as does the deepest interior (often
called *mental*) prayer. And if this mood of humility, of yielding, of utter openness to what is there (to which the wide-
open shutter of our attention is directed), is absent in mental
prayer, then mental prayer can be as mechanical, routine,
and fruitless as the most shabbily rattled off spoken prayer.

The Christian world continues to be full of people who

repeat spoken prayers slowly, attentively, who pause a little from time to time, and who find their devotion to God renewed by means of such spoken prayer. A great spiritual guide declares, "Many people who practice vocal prayer are, without their knowing how, raised by God to a high state of contemplation. . . . I knew [one] who could only make a vocal prayer, yet, while keeping to this, she enjoyed all the rest as well. Unless she used oral prayer, her thoughts wandered to an unbearable extent—yet I wish we all made such mental prayer as she did! . . . I found that she enjoyed pure contemplation while saying the Our Father [Lord's Prayer], . . . I even envied her such vocal prayer."[16] And in the same set of addresses to her colleagues, this guide remarks, "To prove to you that vocal prayer, made perfectly, brings with it no small profit, I may tell you that it is quite possible, while you are reciting the Lord's Prayer or some other prayer (if you say it well), that God may raise you to perfect contemplation."[17]

It is of first importance to note how carefully this promise on spoken prayer is qualified: "if you make it well." Making it well means to make it with the whole attention of the heart: not to hurry—to pause, to be open, to use vocal prayer only as a riverbed into which the water of life can be flowed. Making prayer well also means to make it without stubbornly continuing—at any price—the spoken prayer. Are there not occasions when we can recall going on speaking when we knew well enough that we had finished, and that what we were saying was no longer relevant? We have been sorted out, listened to, even spoken to during the flood of our own speaking. But when we "make it well," the spoken prayer may become a form of deeply interior prayer and be carried out with the receptive and expectant openness of mental prayer. When this occurs, the prior condition of attention and intent that marks both the spoken and the mental prayer is fulfilled and the wall between them disappears.

But can a sixteenth-century witness speak to our time? We might prefer to listen to Simone Weil, a twentieth-century French woman who died in exile in Britain in 1943 at the age of thirty-four, speaking of the infinite possibilities that lie in the use of such a vocal prayer as the Our Father, if it is used as a vehicle of absolute attention to God:

> A week afterwards I began the vine harvest. I recited the "Our Father" in Greek every day before work and I repeated it often in the vineyard.
>
> Since that time I have made a practice of saying it through once each morning with absolute attention. If during the recitation my attention wanders or goes to sleep, in the minutest degree, I begin again until I have once succeeded in going through it with absolutely pure attention. . . .
>
> The effect of this practice is extraordinary and surprises me every time, for, although I experience it each day, it exceeds my expectation at each repetition. . . . Sometimes, also, during this recitation or at

other moments, Christ is present with me in person, but his presence is
infinitely more real, more moving, more clear than on that first occa-
sion when he took possession of me.[18]

Although vocal prayer, audible or silent, is often referred
to as an intermediate grade of prayer, it has a way of involving us, of warming us up, of gently laying hold of our reti-
cent physical apparatus and focusing it upon God. It also is
useful to many in resisting the distractions that beset us in
mental prayer. There is a naturalness about our talking to
God—about getting out into spoken language those things
that have been churning about within us—that commends
spoken prayer to the worship of the millions.

There is the same value in set, spoken prayers repeated
from memory such as the Lord's Prayer or some collect from
A Guide to Prayer for All God's People[19] or *The Book of Com-*
mon Prayer.[20] One may repeat over and over again some
classic phrase like Dean Sperry's favorite prayer of the
Breton fisherman, "O God, thy sea is so great, and my boat is
so small"; or George MacDonald's simple, "O God"; or the
prayer of the publican in the New Testament, "God, be
merciful to me a sinner" (Luke 18:13).

Spoken prayer may be a spontaneous outpouring, or it
may be a prayer repeated from memory or read from a lit-
urgy or from a book of worship. Lancelot Andrewes,[21] a
contemporary of Shakespeare and King James I, prepared
his own book of daily prayers in order to enable his long

morning and evening vigils to search every facet of his soul, and draw within his ken the needs of all the people among whom he was living. Others in our time have found that the preparation and use of such a prayer guide for themselves has been a most helpful exercise.

There are those who find spoken prayer useful, not in place of mental or silent prayer, but as the opening movement that leads on into mental prayer, or as a means of rallying or refocusing a sequence of silent prayer that may have grown scattered. I once listened to an organ tuner who stood as far away from the church organ as he could get and called back directions to his colleague who handled the tuning wrenches. When the tone was unclear to him, he ordered the tuner to drop an octave and, when the proper tone was reached, he called out, "Now go back up again." The use of spoken prayer in rallying the prayer of silence may not be so different from "dropping an octave" until attention is again correctly focused.

SILENT PRAYER *and* WAITING *on* GOD

In most mature persons, spoken prayer at some point gives way to silent prayer, to mental prayer, to a waiting on God. Let us, therefore, explore the use of mental prayer. Perhaps there is no simpler way to describe mental prayer than "putting God at the center of attention." If we are not audibly speaking out our prayer, the query at once arises, "Doesn't the mind wander?" I recall a story of a Hasidic Jew who was explaining to another how you could discover with certainty whether or not a pious rabbi was a true zaddik (a spiritually enlightened one). It was pointed out that one needed only ask him what to do about wandering thoughts, about distractions in prayer. If he answered, he was clearly not a zaddik!

Few of the Christian masters of the spiritual life have been so elevated and hence so oblivious to distractions in prayer. Teresa of Ávila confesses, "My mind wandered about like an insane person from room to room." But with her customary sanity she adds in another place, "We are bound to pray with attention, and may God grant that . . . we may succeed . . . without wandering thoughts. I sometimes suffer from them, and I find that the best remedy is to keep my mind fixed on Him to Whom my words are addressed."[22] Few of us are zaddiks, so distractions are, and are likely to remain, an inevitable part of our life of mental prayer. Someone has remarked that falling in the water does not drown us. It is staying there that does it.

DEALING with DISTRACTIONS in PRAYER

What, then, are these distractions? Where do they come from? Is there a rule of prayer for dealing with them? There are for us all a mass of external distractions—sounds, sights, smells—which almost inevitably bombard our senses when we seek to pray, and which demand our attention. In our noisy world there is almost no hiding place that will not be under attack. But outer distractions are relatively easy to deal with. The first counsel is to accept them as a part of the scenery and not to fight angrily against them. To battle them or to be bitterly resentful of them is to conclude your prayer then and there! Some have found it helpful to pray them as ejaculations directly into their prayer: "O God, may my soul reach out for you with the swiftness of that whining jet that has just hurtled past," or "O God, reveal to me the inner counterpart of this massive outer power that has just passed by," and then to continue quietly with their prayer. An accent on the positive was perfectly expressed by words already quoted, "I find that the best remedy is to keep my mind fixed on Him to Whom my words are addressed." In other words, when distractions appear, remember afresh into Whose Presence you have come.

The inner distractions—the wandering thoughts—are much more difficult to manage than those which come from without, but the same twin counsels hold for them. *Accept them,* salute them, acknowledge them as a part of yourself that is quite naturally present. And having done this, let them remain with you, and turn quietly and calmly to "look over the shoulders" of these distractions, to look to God who is your real object of attention.

Two further things remain to be added. If the same distraction, the same thought persists or keeps recurring, stop for a moment and examine it. Ask yourself, "Is it simply the continuation of the busy click-click of my uncollected life, or is it some unfinished business I am bent on avoiding? Is it some unfaced obligation? Is it perhaps some sin that I have been asking as Augustine did to be 'taken from me, but not yet'?" You might even ask yourself, "What is this distraction, in its persistent recurrence, trying to say to me? Is it something that should be faced in this time of prayer?"

There is a Jewish suggestion that distractions in prayer are blemished deeds in our lives that push their way into prayer in expectation of the blessing that is to come. The distractions hope, by crowding in here, to be redeemed, to be hallowed. This notion goes so far as to regard distractions in prayer as the garment by which God conceals God's self as we approach God in prayer. Such an idea is akin to the one already suggested, namely, that we accept and befriend these distractions and use them in our prayer.

The other counsel is intimately linked to this: it bids us not to be seriously deterred by these supplicants for our attention, but to move on into our prayer. If there is something in them that seems to need longer consideration, a note can be made of it (even a written note, if it will free the mind more fully of the strain of remembering), but now is not the time to pursue interruptions. Now is the time for attention to God.

CHAPTER TWO

TO PRAY IS to CHANGE

In one of the Ajunta caves in mid-India, there is a painting of the young Buddha standing at a parting of the ways. In one of his hands he holds a model of his father's palace to which he is heir and with which go honor, wealth, family, and power. In the other hand he holds the lotus flower, symbol of the call to inner transformation. He must decide between these two, the palace or the lotus.

The contemporary Western reaction to this painting would probably be that the choice it presents is surely much too extreme. "Why can he not have both the palace and the lotus?" Why not do as the pious Emperor Asoka of India and the saintly King Louis of France did, who stayed in their palaces yet took the way of the lotus? "Surely," our contemporaries might say, "in our day we have outmoded any such radical decision as the Buddha's."

The Christian Gospels do not encourage anyone to believe that he or she can choose both the palace and the lotus: both mammon and God (Matthew 6:24). The Gospels are for men and women of free hearts and free wills who must decide for themselves as to where they will bestow their love and allegiance. The Gospels give few particulars as to conduct and choices; they give, rather, the basic principles that each person must apply for him- or herself. They only lay the pruning saw at the foot of the tree. The Gospels confront us with One who pierces us by his bottomless love and caring, One who compels us to decide for ourselves what in our lives is incongruous with his love.

TO COME NEAR to GOD IS to CHANGE

"To come near to God is to change" is a profound Christian statement of a great truth. And the most open way to "come near to God" is prayer. Emily Herman, in her thoroughly reliable book *Creative Prayer*[1] entitles the key chapter "From Self to God." If my prayer is real, my surface self, my ego, my *persona,* must decrease and he must increase in me. I dare not stay as I am and come near to such a love as his. I could not bear it. The many hucksters in me—the mean, demanding deceivers—are put to confusion by such a love.

The Gospel record puts the choice before me in many

different ways, but in none more searchingly than in what Jesus invites me to do about the pearl of great price (Matthew 13:45–46). The perverse notion once occurred to me that this parable might have been put in terms of an auction, perhaps even of a "Dutch auction" where the auctioneer places an absurd price on the object, in this case the pearl, and then gradually scales the price down, until he reaches a figure low enough to find a buyer. I have even pictured myself in the crowd at this auction, anxiously waiting to see what is to happen. "Is there a chance that the pearl of great price might get down into my modest purchasing range?"

I once saw in the museum of modern art at Lawrence College in Appleton, Wisconsin, a contemporary painting of an auction sale. In it the figures were gathered eagerly around an auction platform and the heads of all but one were blurred, each having, not a single face, but many faces. Only the figure of a child had a single face.

I wonder how many faces I might have if the auction were to be a matter of the sale of this pearl. I might think, "Is this last-named price as low as it will go?" "If I do not buy now, will the auctioneer stop the sale at this point, as he is entitled to do, under these rules, and put the pearl back into the vault?" "Shall I bid now or wait a little longer in the hope of a further reduction or, if I do, may not another snatch the pearl at the present price?" "Is the pearl really cheap enough so that my resources will not be seriously taxed if I raise my hand and give the signal that I will buy?" "After all, I have managed until now on synthetic, manufactured pearls. Why should I not go on in this way a while longer?" "How much, after all, do I really want this pearl of great price?" What a contrast my many, contorted, anxious, calculating, bargaining faces would present to that of the single-faced child!

But all of this imaginative embroidering of the parable of the pearl of great price into an auction sale has no ground in the Gospels. For there is no hint there that God is either an auctioneer or that he sells by the descending scale of a "Dutch auction." The Gospel parable gives me two choices. I may sell what I have and buy the pearl in a single transaction, or I may turn away and ignore the whole matter for the present. If I really engage in prayer, "the business of businesses" as medieval writer and monk Bernard of Clairvaux called it, I really awaken to the love with which I am encompassed, and the alternative disappears. There is no middle ground, and I must buy "the pearl of great price," cost what it may. Methodist preacher Russell Maltby knew this and said, "When we go into God's presence it must be a surrender."[2] Søren Kierkegaard bluntly calls prayer "a silent surrendering of everything to God." For good measure, Kierkegaard adds the further observation, "In thy nature and in mine and in that of every [person], there is something He would do away with."[3]

PRAYER *and the* CHAMBER *of* LOVING SCRUTINY

In the moment that we sense in prayer the sweep of God's love, a light is cast upon our own condition revealing us to ourselves as no amount of introspection can do. No amount of considering what we think of ourselves, what our friends think of us, or what our enemies say of us is even faintly comparable to this self-revelation that comes from prayer. It is this chamber of loving scrutiny that Blaise Pascal speaks of when he says that all the troubles that come to people in this world come from their not being willing to stay in their own rooms quietly.[4] If we dare to stay in this chamber—aware of our shortcomings in the Light of God's loving presence— both the revelation of what must be put right and the strength to put it right are given to us. "[The one] who shows a [person] his [or her] sin is the same that takes it away,"[5] declares George Fox. Both the pain and the healing are ministered to us within those chamber walls. But chambers are not all alike.

I recall an elderly woman's telling a group, at the opening of a religious retreat, of her impressive apartment that looked so elegant and orderly and well kept in the parts where guests were permitted to circulate. "But," she confessed, "I've got a room in my apartment that I lock up and permit no one to enter, and it is in the most frightful state of confusion and disorder and chaos." A look of understanding spread over many faces there that evening, for they, too, had a "room," often more than one, that would not stand scrutiny.

In the lives of those who seek to enter the chamber of prayer, there are also "locked rooms," and the keys are often tightly held. There is a story of Mother Angélique Arnauld's reform of the seventeenth-century women's religious order of Port Royal in France, which, in the century preceding, had become very relaxed. She asked the nuns to give up to her willingly all of the little luxuries with which their indulgent families had surrounded them, and she warned them that the intercessory power of the cloister's life of prayer would remain weak until all had fully complied. After the reform seemed completed, the power was still absent until one afternoon one of the sisters pressed into Mother Angélique's hand a secret garden's key that she had kept back. Only then did the surge of power enter the group.

There are the closed rooms of personal hates and fears that doctors have recently discovered and that they try to open with the query, "*Who* is the matter with you?" They know that hate is a prolonged form of suicide. There are the closed rooms of stubborn ambitions, doggedly clung to, that have warped the lives of mates and families. There is the locked room of lovelessness between husband and wife, accepted as unchangeable. There are for us, too, varying species of the fastidious scruple that plagued even a saint like Francis of Assisi. He confessed that he used to ride miles out of his way to avoid passing a leper because he could not abide the stench. Then one day, on the way back from Rome, a leper sprang into the road to beg alms. Francis spurred his horse round him and rode fast to get away from the sickening intrusion. But at a point he stopped his horse, turned him round, returned to the spot, leapt down, embraced the leper, and gave him all that was in his purse.

There is the realization that until now "I have followed with my body the pillar of cloud by day and the pillar of fire by night—but my mind is still in Egypt." There are the wallows of self-pity and self-justification. "To be undervalued in the least is unbearable to us,"[6] notes Teresa. Often there is the unwillingness to accept our own self and, for better or for worse, to live with this self as "one of the least of these" who needs befriending.

We need go no further. Sin, the slug in the soul, the ocean of darkness, the attempt at self-sufficiency, the artful thousand-headed dispersion of ourselves that would maneuver us to escape ever being willing to enter that single chamber, is deeply imbedded within us. Perhaps that is enough to say. But in the chamber of prayer where we become aware of the piercing love of God, in the light of his love, we are brought with an unflinching clarity to see that "I have a closed room" and "I have a hidden key." To come near to a God of revealing love is to change.

A woman once told me of visiting the marketplace in a provincial town in Mexico and of seeing there a Mexican peasant who had brought in his produce in a carrier on his back and had sold it. He then moved about with his little five-year-old daughter hoping that he might be able to buy the wooden pail he needed with the few centavos he had gotten for his vegetables. While the father was selecting a pail, the little daughter stopped at a gaudy stall where a woman placed in her hands a bright parasol with a painted paper top. She raised and lowered it for the child, and the little girl held it up to her father with pleading eyes. He now had bought the pail and had no money left. He slowly shook his head and the little girl gave back the parasol to the woman, ran swiftly to her father, took his hand, and they went off together.

A great confession speaks of prayer as raising our desires to God to see if they are agreeable to God. In the vigil of prayer, there frequently comes what the Quakers call a "stop in the mind" about specific things which, until then, had been taken for granted as acceptable, or at least as passing a minimal *nihil obstat* (nothing against). An honest little girl who prayed each night was asked if God had given her an answer to what she had asked him, and her instant reply was, "Yes. God said 'No.'"

PRAYER *and the* COST *of* RENEWAL

This growing awareness of incongruity, this sorrowing for sin, this increasing readiness to take his hand and go off together (in the words of *The Cloud of Unknowing,* to "take God as He is, flat and plain as a plaster and lay it to thy sick self as thou art . . . to bear up thy sick self unto Gracious God as He is"), is a movement in all real prayer and makes of prayer more than a confessional chamber. It is rather a return to the house of renewal.

My great-grandfather built a largely self-contained village in northern Michigan, complete with lumber mill, shops, houses, and barns. He had in it a smith's shop with anvil and forge and a smith who could mend almost any ordinary iron implement that was broken. It was simply a matter of putting the broken parts into the hot furnace and then, when they were red-hot, of putting them on the anvil and hammering them into shape again. Is it any wonder that, with such a shop and such a smith at hand, there was present among these villagers a sense that even the worst break was healable, or that there was a readiness to go about the day's work with a fresh feeling of assurance and inner security? But in order to be repaired, it must be noted, the iron had to go back to the smith, become fire-hot and malleable, and be hammered back to its original shape. It could be restored at no less price. All the great teachers of prayer remind us of the necessity of returning for reshaping. St. John of the Cross said, "Learn that the flame of everlasting love doth burn ere it transforms." Augustine Baker confesses that prayer is "the greatest of all mortifications." It is worth noting, however, that the greatest pain comes from the tightness of our grip on that which holds us back.

There are many popularizers of prayer in our day who seem to describe prayer as a kind of swift gimmick for attaining a well-adjusted personality or success in business or a career. They depict it as though it were a type of detachable auxiliary motor of the kind Europeans buy to attach to their bicycles so that they will no longer have to pump the pedals on journeys that have long since become routine as far as direction is concerned. What a contrast between this idea of prayer and that of the masters who compel us to see in prayer a "continual conversion." Père Jean-Nicholas Grou tells us, "The Holy Spirit will either control your actions or cease to govern your prayers." *To come near to God is to change.*

WHY DO WE STOP OUR PRAYERS?

I have always quickened to Lawrence Housman's inspired reference to St. Francis as "a saint who made goodness attractive." I have glowed at what Russell Maltby included in his "Precepts for Preachers": "You preach the gospel; there-fore, no demand without the gift; no diagnosis without the cure. One word about sin; ten for the Saviour."[7] I have also felt deep gratitude to Olive Wyon for including in her mov-ing book *On the Way* the reminiscences about Bishop Wes-ton of Zanzibar who seemed "not much interested in my sins but spoke to me a great deal about the love of God."[8] I am inwardly certain that the love of God as poured out in Jesus Christ is the primary accent in prayer as elsewhere.

This love can lead to real change. In the presence of this love, a profound awareness of our sins consumes us and changes in our lives take place.

Is it not a dread of this self-awareness and this change that causes each of us to resist the call to continued prayer? Is it not this that causes us to give up vital prayer again and again? Is not this dread the reason that we do not pray? It can be put almost as bluntly as this: we do not pray, or we give up prayer, because a strategist within us knows all about what takes place in this prayer chamber, knows that a drastic change is involved, and senses the threat. This strate-gist therefore routes us around it. If the inner strategist can help it, there is to be no "Blessed are the poor in *self* for they shall see God," no disinfection of the swollen ego. And its ingenuity is beyond description! An old veteran of prayer who knew this inner antagonist well once noted, "One day we are absent because our head aches, the next because it has ached, and three more lest it should ache again."[9]

All of this has been humorously put by C. S. Lewis in his *Screwtape Letters*[10] where the Enemy (Screwtape) is pictured as instructing his nephew, Wormwood, in his work of deceiving people. He warns him to interfere at any price and in any fashion when people start to pray, for real prayer is lethal to "our" (the Enemy's) cause.

It has even more recently been put in the fresh and breezy jargon of Tom Powers, who pictures us surrendering in prayer and then attempting for the rest of the day "to get out of the driver's seat."

> *The monkey really hates this business and will inevitably counterattack on two fronts, first with the tweezers and later on with a wrench. His first tweezer touches . . . are so light and so deft that you have to be an old campaigner to notice what is actually going on. All that a neophyte can observe is that, somehow, in spite of good intentions, he is forgetting to surrender. Automatically, with no conscious knowledge of how it happened, again and again he winds up in the driver's seat and running his own life like a fire engine. So he tried again to surrender, and again, but less often as time goes on.*

Of the monkey wrench, Powers writes:

> *He [the monkey] brings it to bear if and when the tweezers fail . . . if you really do begin to get out of the driver's seat, if the attitude of abandonment begins to become habitual and to involve the heart—then the infernal little chum begins to clobber you with the wrench. . . .*

"What! Are we to have no part in the government of our very own life—none at all? Does God . . . now propose to make a puppet of us? . . . Are we finally to have no privacy, no choice, no adventure, no noble individual and personal striving? . . . We won't have it! That's all. We just will forget all about it and get back to normal, back to sanity, back to real life. . . .

Maybe you think this is a jolly over-portrayal. On the contrary, it is taken right from life, my own and others. And again it is much more likely to happen to you than you can possibly realize until you, yourself, really try to surrender.[11]

We can have our choice of symbols and metaphors and parables, but the situation that they all depict is too real to shrug off. Prayer is a threat to the continued enthronement of our egocentric goals. There is a massive resistance in us to continued prayer. That is why we stop praying, which is natural. It is also why we must ever begin again and again, which is supernatural, of God, and meant to be an instrument of our redemption.

ON ACCEPTING *the* FORGIVENESS *of* GOD

A discussion of Christian prayer that leaves out the final movement of forgiveness would be a travesty. There is nothing that God cannot heal, and God's forgiveness is given before we even approach God. Nowhere is this more tellingly described than in the Old Testament story of the father

King David weeping over his son Absalom who has perhaps come to his death because he did not believe his father could ever forgive his treason: "O my son Absalom, my son, my son Absalom!" (2 Samuel 18:33).

Forgiveness is a condition in which the sin of the past is not altered, nor its inevitable consequences changed. Rather in forgiveness a fresh act is added to those of the past, which restores the broken relationship and opens the way for the one who forgives and the one who is forgiven to meet and communicate deeply with each other in the present and future. Thus, forgiveness heals the past, though the scars remain and the consequences go on. These keep the sinner humble. But now the past can no longer throttle. It is taken into the fresh act of outgoing renewal and there it is healed.

The whole witness of Jesus' life and death is to the unfathomable depths of God's forgiveness. English poet and artist William Blake cites the capacity of Jesus to forgive another, and to reenter vulnerably into the deepest relation with another, as the strongest evidence of his being God in the flesh. For only so could someone be truly able to forgive others.

There is, however, a condition for receiving God's gift of forgiveness. Humankind must be willing to accept it. Absurd as this may seem, there are few who will believe in and accept the forgiveness of God so completely as to let God bury their sin in God's forgiving mercy; or who, having once accepted that forgiveness, will leave their sin with God forever. They are always reopening the vault where they have deposited their sin, and are forever asking to have it back in order to fondle it; reconstruct, query, or worry over it; wear it inwardly. Thus their sin ties them to the past and finally dooms their lives in both the present and the future.

I knew a man who, in his wife's lifetime, had fallen into some personal practices that led him after her death to believe that he had failed the noble character of her faith in him. She was gone, and he saw no way of asking her forgiveness. He had been going over the framework of these sins for a decade. The events in his past loomed up and held him back from a life of inward peace in his advanced years. Out of a heart of despair, he asked another whether he believed that God could forgive even this sin. In a time of prayer he later found that God could, but that he had first of all to *accept* God's forgiveness, to deposit this structure of sin with God and forever forgo asking for it again.

Quaker Gerald Heard once told a group at Wainright House to note that when a great whore had confessed all to François de Sales, she fainted, and François de Sales knelt before her as if she were a holy one who had been utterly purified by God.

The forgiveness of God, the absolution, the utter blotting out of our sin and the restoration to wholeness is also found in the chamber of prayer Pascal spoke of. Forgiveness, however, can only be received by those who will accept its conditions. To be cleansed and to accept the cleansing, then to move on into the present and the future as a forgiven and restored one, is the gift of the deepest prayer. The query that might be placed over the door of the Pascalian chamber would be, "Are you willing to accept the forgiveness of God?"

PRAYER *and* ADORATION

Von Hügel once declared, "Any religion that ignores the adoration of God is like a triangle with one side left out." It would be hard to come to any other conclusion about a form of prayer that left out the whole dimension of gratitude and veneration. There are many people in our time who simply have no conception of what adoration is or what part it must take in the practice of prayer. If they conceive of it at all, they associate it with elaborate ceremonial worship, with candles burning before an altar. With a repugnance almost worthy of the Old Testament prophets' denouncing burnt offerings in favor of sound ethical action, they will have none of this ceremonial nonsense. What then is adoration, and what is its role in the practice of prayer?

There is a spot some two thousand feet above Darjeeling, India, where a visit before daybreak, if the weather is favorable, may bring you the slow emergence of the whole Himalaya range from Kanchenjunga to Mt. Everest. To look at that immaculate, glittering sweep of white radiance is to have something happen in you. You do not want to climb the range, to photograph it, to paint it, to survey it, to quarry it, to mine it, to own it. Your one longing is to be left in quiet before it to marvel that anything on this earth could be so wonderful. Adoration is something like that. There is an ancient Hindu prayer that says only, "Wonderful, Wonderful, Wonderful."

There are times when we go on a long tramp with someone for whom we greatly care. There has been talk, but it has now faded, and we can stalk along mile after mile together without a word but in perfect communication—each glad for the other's presence, each glad the other is alive, each grateful to be the other's friend, each feeling understood, each cherishing the other. This experience, too, throws light on another facet of the nature of adoration.

A young man who has taken his parents largely for granted can discover someday with a blinding flash just what their caring and willingness to put nothing ahead of his opportunities have meant to him. He may be flooded with a surge of gratitude that they are his and he is theirs. He may feel in that moment a hard knot in him break, and find himself, perhaps for the first time, presented with the gift of tears. Adoration has in it something like that.

The adoration of God in prayer is a mixture of gratitude

and reverence and awe. It is not only gratitude for God's gifts but for God's *self,* for God's constancy and unplumbable mystery that seems always to haunt the countless expressions of God's intimate concern. It is not reverence for something that *ought* to be respected, but a firsthand feeling of being moved to the core, of being made to feel abased and yet drawn up to the pinnacle of one's being simply by the fact of this Presence. It is not an awe that is marked by the glandular disturbances characteristic of physical fear. Rather it is a sense of being swept both qualitatively and quantitatively by that which one's slender vessel cannot contain but before which it can be set in the highest vibration. Adoration in prayer is a time for God alone. George MacDonald has it in a single line, "It is not what God can give us, but God that we want." The peasant who confessed that in his prayer "God just looks down at me and I look up at him" witnesses to the same mood.

SOME POSITIVE SIDE EFFECTS *of* ADORATION

A curious paradox often occurs in the prayer of adoration. The time when we turn away from our petitions and intercessions, our problems and our desires, and simply sit or kneel in thankfulness in God's presence has a strangely ordering effect upon all that we are and all that we are carrying. There is a story of a Harvard student who had a personal problem that he seemed utterly incapable of unraveling. A roommate suggested that he take it to the renowned preacher Phillips Brooks, and finally, overcoming his shyness at troubling so great a man with such a relatively insignificant matter, the student got an appointment and spent half an hour with him. When he returned, the roommate wanted to hear how Phillips Brooks had resolved his friend's problem. The problem, as a matter of fact, had never even been mentioned, he reported, but in the course of the visit, the way to resolve it had become clear.

I once talked with the Polish wife of the biographer of Ramana Maharshi, a country Brahmin, whom many in India found to be a veritable window to God. She told me how she used to come down to Southern India from Calcutta, torn with personal problems, and how she would go over and sit in the big living room of the ashram with Ramana Maharshi. She did not talk with him, but simply spent an hour or two quietly in his presence, while others were coming and going. That was enough. She found the knots unraveling, the things that had to be done resolved, the divisions in her healed, and she left in peace.

Adoration is not for the resolution of problems, yet it often brings to a thankful and reverential person an unexpected blessing. In the practice of prayer there should be ample time for adoration.

CHAPTER THREE

———•—•———

THE POWER
of
PRAYER

In the month of December children are known to prepare lists, not of the presents they mean to give, but of the presents they would like to receive. They are often most ingenious in the ways they find of circulating these lists.

There are expositors of Christian prayer who look upon the prayer of petition, of bluntly and brazenly asking for things, as if it were in this Christmas-list category. They denounce it as vulgar and unworthy of an adult who has really learned the nature of Christian prayer. They maintain that we ought only to seek God and God's way for us and ought not ply God for gifts. There is a Sufi prayer that says:

> *If I seek thee to avoid Hell, burn me,*
>
> *If I seek thee in the hope of Paradise, exile me;*
>
> *But if I seek Thee for Thyself alone,*
>
> *Turn not Thy holy countenance from me.*

Bernard of Clairvaux also distinguishes between those who love God for God's gifts and those who love God for God's self alone.

But when it comes to the matter of petitionary prayer, of bringing our personal desires and needs before God, Jesus seems to be on the side of the children, both in his personal practice of asking for specific things and of encouraging his companions to do the same.

The saints and the whole Christian community have always used petition freely. The privilege of petition is a part of the bounty given to those of the kingdom of God. God does not seek to direct our attention away from this life, from God's creation, but leaves us involved in it to the hilt. God would not have us retreat into some stoical condition of resignation and invulnerability as far as this world is concerned. As preacher P. T. Forsyth put it, "If you may not come to God with the occasions of your private life and affairs, then there is some unreality in the relation between you and [God]."[1]

ON AUTHENTIC ASKING in PRAYER

How then are we to distinguish those petitions that are simply a kind of mobilization of God toward our egoistic goals, a using of God as we would use an auxiliary bicycle motor, from the free petitionary relationship into which God has invited God's children? I strongly suspect that God is far less fastidious in this matter than are these sophisticated expositors of Christian prayer. There is a sense in which Harry Emerson Fosdick and P. T. Forsyth are profoundly right in defining prayer respectively as humanity's "dominant desire" and our "ruling passion," and therefore seeing the whole of people's desire as prayer whether they acknowledge it as such or not. If this be so, then all of us are in a sense praying all the time, in our ambitions, in our basic longings, and in our vital principles. We are always focused either on God or on God's adversary.

If my consciously directed prayer to God is, in the deepest sense, the focus of my ruling passion, and its focus is upon God, then the most miserable one-knee-only prayer that would use and exploit God to advance the cause of the other unbent knee is still a coming within God's field of force. It may be that by coming into this field of force, no matter how inadequately, I will discover that my prayer undergoes a change. In other words, God will not be mocked. Let a person begin in prayer where he or she is, and that means anywhere, with any problem, with any desire. If what that person asks for has him or her in its grip, that means that God can meet that person there. If he or she has a ruling passion to be liked by others, to be selected to an important post, to be able to hold a marriage together, to recover the confidence of a son or daughter, why should this not come squarely into prayer? We can begin anywhere in petitionary prayer.

Social reformer Jane Addams was once addressing a group of women in Chicago, most of them first-generation immigrants, who were having a hard time holding the respect and understanding of their own daughters. She told them that when their adolescent daughters came home from school and wanted to talk to them, they had better stop everything and listen, even if the cake burned in the oven! "Because," she added, "if you don't listen to the little things first, the big things won't come out."

It is similar with our prayers. God has all of the time in the world, and has great patience with the little things with which we often shyly begin. The only condition that needs to be made about starting anywhere in petitionary prayer is that we stay on in prayer until the little things give way to the big things. We must stay on until we wrestle these trifling matters out and until we are prepared to consider at least the intimations that may come to us as to what is to be done.

There is a question that arises at once. Is not the prayer of petition one thing for those who have not wholly committed their lives to God and an entirely different thing for those who are at least approaching the condition of Teresa of Ávila who sensed God's saying to her "that it was time she took upon her His affairs as if they were her own, and that He would take her affairs upon Himself"?[2] Do we of the mixed station, we who are not fully committed, have any such right to turn to God in the desperateness of our need and burst out in a begging prayer? Consider the account of a confessed atheist who, in the agony of shock therapy, cried out to God for mercy and strength; or a soldier for whom religion had had no meaning who, when crouched in a trench with shrapnel shells being lobbed all about him, prayed to God for his life; or a graduate student, faced with the most critical examination of his career and tempted to postpone it and flee, but who found himself suddenly upon his knees before God; or a despairing woman who saw her marriage breaking up, who fell to her knees and cried out, "O God, be merciful to me a sinner and, if it be possible, show me the way back into the marriage relationship we once knew together—or into something even better." Are the desperate prayers of such uncommitted ones legitimate?

This question about petitionary prayer for the committed and for the uncommitted is a searching one. Its answer, insofar as anyone can give an answer in so great a mystery as prayer, is in precisely the same direction as that given to the initial objection that the prayer of petition might be used to exploit God for our own ends. Here again, God is, I believe, far less squeamish than God's theological bodyguard. Let us remember the thief on the cross who begged for mercy and received it immediately, and in just that instantaneous sequence.

The question nevertheless is not an idle one to be dismissed with such an example. The prayer of the thief on the cross, in his extremity, showed an inner acknowledgment and an utter willingness, even before he received Jesus' confirmation, to be joined to the redemptive company as his life was ebbing away (Luke 23:39–43).

The real shaft of the question takes us to what, in these extremities, really happens in the person who prays. Is the person only out to get safely through the extremity, or is he or she prepared, impelled by the extremity, to turn around, to discover and move into a new dimension of life?

When people in extremity finally go to a psychotherapist, they often describe their symptoms. They are not able to sleep. A twitch is developing in a left shoulder. A quiver has come in a right hand that makes the person unable to hold a teacup without spilling or to eat soup in company. They may well be humiliated to be in the presence of a therapist at all. They may try to make clear to the doctor that they want swift relief from these symptoms—and the less messing about in their private lives the better. If they persist in this approach to their extremity, it is obvious that they will be sealed off from help. Quite as effectively, the person who seeks only to be rid of the extremity through petitionary prayer would seal him- or herself off from divine therapy.

But on the other hand, the very seriousness of symptoms may drive the persons to make a full disclosure of their condition in great openness. A rustic once suggested that "prayers that has no need in 'em has no suction power." If "God is where a person lets God in," if, as Meister Eckhart puts it, "our opening and his entry is one breath," then even the anguished prayer of the uncommitted can be a moment of opening, a threshold of commitment.

BEGINNING WHERE YOU ARE

There is a closely allied question about the rightness of taking unworthy complaints, desires, and demands into God's presence in prayer. Suppose that you long to be promoted, or you want to be chosen as the representative of your group to an important assembly, or you are a prisoner of war in exile and yearn to be in the next group of releases. If this is your dominant desire, it is in a certain sense your unconscious prayer, whether you utter it or not. If *beginning* where you are is right, and you hold this dominant desire up openly in prayer to God, is this a travesty of prayer?

It is well to remember that if this is an act of Christian prayer, you hold up your desires before a God of love. You hold them up in the name and in the spirit of that Crucified One, and it is amazing the sorting over, the sifting power that takes place there—if you stay on your knees. If the prayer is more than a "God always agrees with me," if it is more than the holding up of a filled-in check for God to sign, then you can in truth begin anywhere. "Do not use Christ," says P. T. Forsyth, "simply to countersign your egoist petition by a closing formula ['in Christ's name']. . . . Prayer in Christ's name is prayer for Christ's object—for His kingdom."[3]

How amazingly the petitions with which we enter prayer are refashioned in the very prayer itself. You have come filled with a sense of injustice, of self-pity. You say, "I am a special case, but no one treats me with any special consideration. I have been overlooked, ignored, neglected, insulted; my neighbor has been singled out, appreciated, honored, and exalted. This is too much, God, and I cannot bear it." The presence of the Crucified One provides a magnificent context in which to pour out such prayers. If they are on your heart they belong in your prayer.

In Christ's presence you can plead your case with the most measured eloquence, until finally he listens you into silence, into humiliation, into humility, and at last you come into some faint splash of the deep sanity that recalls you to what you are on earth for, that puts these petitions in the revitalized awareness of your real objectives, that turns your heartburn into heartease and makes you ready for the next assignment. What a tragedy if you should have kept these surface urgencies of your life away from conscious prayer where they were lifted out of the unconscious depths and subjected to the divine winnowing and faced once and for all.

But the petitions may not concern moving from down-and-out to up-and-on in this world. They may be prayers to resist a temptation or to give yourself more completely into God's hands. The prayer may even be a request for some crosses to help you test and strengthen your devotion to God. It is in prayer that you can face temptation and recognize your peculiar weakness at the moment it threatens to overwhelm you. If we stay in prayer we are given the strength needed to refuse the temptation so that we are no longer helplessly vulnerable to it.

Meister Eckhart said boldly, "The kingdom of heaven is only for the perfectly dead"—dead to self, that is. While I know myself excluded from the kingdom on any such terms, I nevertheless know what it is to die a little death to a given temptation faced in prayer. I can occasionally even discover in prayer the personal meaning of a certain temptation and how to turn it into something creative for me and for others who are concerned.

On the matter of a prayer for greater devotion and for crosses, I may find myself referred to the domestic department when I had intended to be applying for dramatic foreign service. There is a ditty that runs,

I thought I'd buy a nice hair shirt
To make me feel ecstatic,
"Why not," the salesman made reply,
"Try one from your own attic?"

ON HAVING "FAR TOO MUCH SENSE *for* EVERYTHING WE DO"

Your petition may more often be a prayer for guidance. You may in prayer go over the day ahead as far as you can predict it: each expected visit, each difficult decision, the special letters that are to be written. It may be a prayer for guidance in the profession or work you are moving toward, the mate you will choose, the way you will spend a sum of money, the use of a period of free time that you have at your disposal. The fact that you pray about these things does not exclude your getting the maximum help available from other sources. It does, however, supply a major factor in your decision making. There is a line that says, "Keep open, oh, keep open . . . my eyes, my mind, my heart,"[4] and prayer does just that. It keeps you open for a leading. Teresa of Ávila has said that "most of us have far too much sense for everything we do." By bringing all your affairs into your life of prayer, you keep the "sense," the hard, worldly wisdom, in its place and the tender openness is given its way. This does not mean that you claim that the content of your prayer is infallible, nor that your responsibility for your decision is removed. It does mean that another factor has been permitted to enter and to operate and that wondrous things happen.

DOES PRAYER CHANGE THINGS?

A shrewd critic might note that until now this account of the prayer of petition has stayed on relatively safe ground. It has dealt chiefly with prayer's effect in bringing us ultimately to a condition of yielding, of adjusting ourselves to the inevitable. We have not really faced the bald claim insisted on by many committed Christian veterans that petitionary prayer changes *events*. To put it bluntly, they seem to believe that the prayer of petition, if it is persisted in, will wear God down into doing the yielding, so that they will get their petition. For them, God answers prayer, things happen, miracles still take place, and we live in a dynamic universe where prayer is a factor in effecting changes. It is as simple as that for them.

This claim on the part of these bold, committed Christians, when it is fairly made, does not deny that these prayers must be made in Jesus' name and after his nature. They are aware of the conditions of the New Testament promise, "If you abide in me, and my words abide in you, ask whatever you will, and it shall be done for you" (John

15:7). This qualification excludes any reducing of prayer to a form of magic where it can be used as a secret weapon to advance our egoistical purposes—either privately or corporately. Nor does this qualification deny the final bending before the mystery of God's purposes as in the Gethsemane prayer, "not my will, but thine, be done" (Luke 22:42). It does not encourage snake handling to dazzle the multitude, nor does it look with contempt upon science and medicine for what they, by the costly and sacrificial intensity of their scrutiny, have been able to teach us about our world and our bodies.

After all of this is said, however, these Christians do insist that prayer changes things. Jesus has encouraged them, they say, to expect and to receive what they need from God's treasury—even if this treasury may be money or services stored in the pockets and persons of people everywhere.

To call on the Lord's treasury presupposes that those who pray have first done everything in their own power to meet the need. Then, "having done all" (Ephesians 6:13), they need not only "stand" but are encouraged to beg of God what is still lacking (Matthew 7:7–11). The vigor of their prayers shows them to be importunate beggars (like the stranger at midnight in Luke 11:5–10), who mean to persist until they prevail. The New Testament encouragement for this kind of persistence until the bread is given or the judgment rendered has not been lost on them (Luke 18:1–8).

PRAYER *and the* DIVINE STRATEGY

Yet in spite of the New Testament parables, is not such persistence a piece of cosmic impertinence? Do these petitioners think they can change God's mind by their dogged picketing? They would, I believe, reject the condemnatory tone of these questions and ask for a better statement of their attitude. When you ask the one whom you are loyally serving for the means of carrying on your service, would that person resent your plea as an effort to "change his mind"? Would that person not rather regard your persistence as a sign of your boundless faith in both his capacity to assist you and his understanding? P. T. Forsyth, like William Temple, has pointed out that God's ultimate purpose is unchanging but God's strategy may vary infinitely. Then could not the presence of a human will expressing in prayer this confidence in this purpose be in itself a significant variable to be taken account of by God in carrying out the ultimate aim? Dorothy Day told how, in order to feed the breadlines in their Catholic Worker Houses of Hospitality in the depth of the depression of the 1930s, the workers made the daily round of every known source of supply, and prayed persistently. She testified that money and supplies came in so that they were never without something to live on and to share. She admitted that the Lord's diet often got a little monotonous—there was the time when they had nothing to eat but leftover cafeteria clam chowder for a fortnight—but they did not starve! Bernardo's Homes for Orphans in Britain, as well as Bodelschwingh's original work with epileptics at Bethel in Germany, were entirely supported in this way. Cyril Powell's book *Secrets of Answered Prayer*[5] presents a striking collection of such authentic instances.

While there has been bogus talk about "prayer prevailing" when instead the help has been wrung from people by fierce and relentless publicity, is it beyond our credibility to believe that all human hearts have an inner window to God through which they are often tendered and made generous? Can we not believe that many are secretly drawn by God to assume the burdens of those in need, to volunteer their services, or to appear at the place and time they are needed? The Christian annals are full of accounts of those who answered such calls.

PRAYER *and the* "LAWS *of* NATURE"

Let us now take the situation to its extreme point. What about prayers for rain? These cannot be passed off by the remark of the New England farmer who prayed, "Thou knowest, O Lord, that what this field needs is not so much rain as a good coat of manure." But the problem is still with us. Is a prayer for rain to be regarded as a pure reversion to magic, and is it to be rejected in our approach to petitionary prayer? I am going to take the liberty of quoting from an earlier writing of mine on this subject, one which I have seen no reason to change.

What about prayers for rain? Those who ask this question usually set up a deep ditch between the psychological and the physical and insist that whereas prayer may affect the psychological, it may never cross the ditch to influence the physical. George Meredith insisted that we ought not to expect God to step in between us and the operation of his laws. In the healing of the sick the boundaries of this ditch have changed somewhat since Meredith's time. Some physicians have begun to admit that what the patient believes profoundly affects his [or her] chances for physical recovery. This has not meant an abandonment of medical science. It has only been a recognition that body and mind are not enemies, but function as a whole, and that the structure of the "laws" that the human being responds to is broader than he [or she], as a doctor, had formerly suspected. In fact the very status of physical laws is at no point so absolute or inexorable as Meredith and his generation believed it. Some of the ablest of scientists are willing to admit that science deals with reality in only one of several possible ways, each of which leaves out something which could be known only by the adoption of a different approach.

We do not know that prayers for rain affect a power that supplies a factor left out by meteorological predictions. Neither do we know that this is not the case. In either event, it implies no abandonment of our active co-operation with our creative stem: the conservation of moisture by the planting of forests, the plowing under of humus matter, the continuing to experiment with the mechanical means of influencing the precipitation of moisture-laden clouds, the improvement of our techniques of irrigation. Prayer is only another form of this same intimate co-operation between us and the stem. If a group of people are suffering from a drought that threatens them with extinction, and if they are people who hold up their every need in prayer, they can and should make no exception of this need. The boundaries of this ditch are yet to be established, and is there not the promise that if you abide in the life "ye shall ask what ye will . . ."? There is, then, no absolute limit that can be placed upon petition. The only limit is [humankind's] need. . . . Faith in God is set prior to faith in prayer, yet given this, you may begin at any point. And those old friends of prayer take their every need into prayer with great ease and confidence.[6]

THE SOCIAL DIMENSION *in* PRAYER: INTERCESSION

Petitionary prayer need not be confined to our own needs. It may focus on the needs of other persons or situations; then it is usually called *intercessory* prayer. There is something startling in the human situation that intercession brings out. Notwithstanding our ultimate aloneness and individuality, evident in the final core of freedom and responsibility in each of us, we are all bound up in the "bundle of the living" (1 Samuel 25:29). And even at the most individual and most free and responsible pinnacle of our being, we are open to being helped and brothered by other souls.

Intercession is the most intensely social act of which the human being is capable. When carried on secretly, it is mercifully preserved from, in fact, almost immunized against, the possible corruptions to which all outer deeds of service for others are subject.

Baron von Hügel once observed that "no one is ever saved alone or by his own efforts." He wrote his beloved niece, Gwendolen Greene, about the costly business of intercession, "I wonder whether you realize a deep, great fact? That souls—all human souls—are interconnected? . . . that we can not only pray for each other, but *suffer for* each other. These long, trying, wakings [what he called his 'white nights'] I was able to offer to God, to Christ for my child [G. G.] that He might ever strengthen, sweeten, steady her in her true, simple, humble love and dependence upon Him. Nothing is more real than this interconnection—this gracious power put by God Himself into the very heart of our infirmities."[7]

The theme of Charles Williams's *Descent into Hell*[8] (considered by many his best novel) is "the substitutionary carrying" in intercessory prayer. In this we costily bear each other in crises and help each other climb the stiles and get over the critical thresholds that we face. In his novel, it is clear that Pauline would never have made it without help from Stanhope.

INTERCESSION *and the* CONTINUOUS SIEGE *of* SOULS

In this ultimate social act of befriending the souls of persons or of reaching for the resolution of a situation from its inside window, there is, however, another factor. In Christian intercessory prayer there is a consciousness that your act of prayer enters into a great sweep of intercession that is already going on. For the agony of Christ that shall last until the end of the world is precisely this intercession for the souls of women and men in the world. This state of loving siege at the inner window never ceases, and when I pray for another, I join with God and Christ and the communion of dedicated souls in something that is already operative. Yet this eternal pleading or redemptive process, if we dare speak of so great a mystery, seems to be aided by—yes, even to require—my prayer, my sacrificial readiness to carry another, and to face the cost of this carrying as the final surge that may liberate the person's soul.

The question arises, however, as to what can be the possible significance of my frail addition to this siege? Is it not, in fact, an arrogant insolence to think that your prayer could matter when all this mighty force has not been sufficient?

We are supplied with no infallible metaphysics of intercessory prayer, and over against such a mystery our conjectures are always outside surmises and no more. Yet it would seem that souls are not only interconnected, but that they are *interconnected in God,* as though the many wicks of our lamps draw their oil from the same full cruse in which they are all immersed.

When Pascal hints of God's having "established prayer to communicate to His creatures the dignity of causality,"[9] is he perhaps expressing in another way the clue that this intercessory path of assisting one another over the critical thresholds has been left open to humankind by God's design? Does it not also imply that your prayers *do* matter, that they are a cosmic fact, that they may tip the balance?

There would seem to be a further confirmation here of the relevance of the earlier suggestion that, *while the ultimate goal of God is constant, the divine strategy of reaching that goal may be swiftly and joyously altered in the light of the occurrence of the costly prayers of committed men and women.*

"WHEN I PRAY, COINCIDENCES HAPPEN"

A Japanese Christian girl, whose family life had been destroyed by her father's drunkenness, set about to intercede for his release from this curse. The passion and persistence of her prayers seemed to reach through to something that plucked his sleeve, drew him to turn around, and purged him of this stubborn addiction. A woman living on the borderline of serious mental illness was held up constantly by the prayers of another and found herself making the grade in spite of periodic threats of relapse. A man in sharp temptation, and with every predilection to succumb, seemed drawn back by the persistent prayers of one who cared for him and for his future. Are these cases merely coincidences? Speaking of his own practice of intercessory prayer, all that William Temple, the late Archbishop of Canterbury, would say on this point was, "When I pray, coincidences happen, and when I do not, they don't." And that is perhaps all that there is to say.

Again queries arise in our minds about a number of facets of such prayer. If prayer has such mysterious power, how can we be sure that we are not back in the realm of magic and witchcraft and that someone may not use prayer for evil ends as a sorcerer was once believed able to use his power? Or still more urgently, how can we be sure that, with the best intention in the world, we are not praying for the wrong thing for the one for whom we make intercession?

In Christian intercessory prayer the same guiding principle spoken of earlier is present: If the prayer is made in the name and after the spirit of Christ, there is, from the very outset, in that continual intercession in which he is taking part a cleansing of the prayer from all wrong intent. The matter of whether or not we are praying for the right thing is always open to that same cleansing. Also, the persistence required in genuine prayer gives to those who use intercessory prayer an additional assurance. If it is true that we are interconnected with other souls in the very life of God, then our prayer, if we stay with it, must be poured through *that life* and be subject to the same winnowing, sorting, and correcting that ordinary petitionary prayer experiences. Here again we can begin anywhere, but we are required to do it in Christ's name and spirit, and to stay on in prayer until things have been worked through. The veterans of prayer who have experienced what happens in such intercession know well enough how often our prayers for others are reshaped. They are refashioned in that living plexus of love through which they must pass to reach those for whom we truly pray.

Of this "perpetual intercession" through which our prayers must pass, P. T. Forsyth once wrote, "Our best prayer, broken, soiled, and feeble as it is, is caught up and made prayer indeed and power with God. This intercession prays for our very prayer, and atones for the sin in it. . . . This is praying 'for Christ's sake.'"[10]

But there is a further query that often haunts intercessory prayer. If it can have such effects, does it not turn those prayed for into maneuvered robots and rob them of their freedom? All that can be said in the face of this mystery is that the freedom to reject, what a friend of mine calls "the freedom to flop," still remains. It seems evident, however, that the attractiveness of the besieging love is increased, and the threshold of resistance to it is correspondingly reduced by such prayers. Often, either consciously or unconsciously, a choice is made by the one who is prayed for to yield to this attraction. If we are to trust philosopher A. N. Whitehead's suggestion that the greatest proof for the reality of the good is the instability of evil, then, certainly, in the intercessory prayers of the committed ones there is a force that adds to that instability, and keeps the way open to change.

THE COST *of* INTERCESSORY PRAYER

When we begin to pray for another, we begin to know and to understand and to cherish him or her as never before. There is a vivid confirmation of Phillips Brooks's well-known word that "If you want to know the worth of a human soul, try to save one." We also begin to realize that such prayer does not come cheaply, and we get a hint of what someone meant when she spoke of "the crucible of divine love."

When I start boldly enough to pray, "O God, may your kingdom come in Mary, and your will be done in Mary," something seems to inquire whether I have not left out something. I begin again, adding this time "be done in Mary *and in me."* I soon discover, too, that it may have to be done "in me" in ways that I have no notion or intention of, before the threshold in Mary is really lowered.

If we want to keep out of personal involvement, intercessory prayer should be instantly scratched from our list; there is nothing that brings us into the scene like intercessory prayer, even when it is done entirely in secret. English leader Oliver Cromwell once said, "We never go so far as when we do not know where we are going," and in intercessory prayer that is exactly our situation. When we begin, we never know what we shall ourselves be brought to if we persist in this prayer. As we set out, something seems to mock us with continual questions that carry in them an intimation of what may be in store for us. "How much do you really care?" "When did this sudden interest in the friend you are praying for arise?" "If there should need to be a drop of blood, of your blood, in this prayer, would you still be for it?" "If it should be substantially more than a drop, what then?"

Alexander Whyte tells with great honesty of a personal experience of one of these inner conversations in the matter of intercession for the physical preservation of the life of a friend.

> [A] dear friend of mine was sick and was seemingly nigh unto death.
> And I was much in prayer for him that he might be spared to his family,
> to his friends and to his great work. And one night as I was in that

intercessory prayer a Voice suddenly . . . said to me—"Are you in
real earnest in what you ask? Or are you uttering, as usual, so many of
your idle words in this solemn matter? Now to prove the sincerity and
the integrity of your love for your friend, and to seal the truth of what
you say about the value of his life, will you give Me and yourself a solid
proof that you are in real earnest in what you say?" "What is the
proof?" I asked, all trembling, and without looking up. And the Voice
said, "Will you consent to transfer to your sick friend the half of your
remaining years? Suppose you have two more years to live and work
yourself, will you give over one of them to your friend? Or if you have
ten years yet before you, will you let your friend have five of them?" I
sprang to my feet in a torrent of sweat. It was a kind of Garden of
Gethsemane to me. But, like [what happened to Jesus at] Gethsemane,
I got strength to say, "Let it be as Thou hast said. Thy will be done.
Not my will but Thine be done." I lay down that never-to-be-forgotten
night with a clean heart and a good conscience as never before both
toward God and toward my much-talented friend. How the matter is to
end I know not. . . . Enough for me and enough for you, that my
story is true and is no idle tale.[11]

In a letter to Baron von Hügel, during his spiritual direction of her life, Evelyn Underhill once wrote about the cost
of intercession: "As to intercession, if I asked myself whether
I could face complete spiritual deprivation for the good of
another: e.g., to effect a conversion, I can't do that yet. So I
have not got real Christian love: and the question is, can one
intercede genuinely for anyone unless ready to pay, if neces-

sary, this price."[12] She received the wise answer from him, that she might go ahead and do what she found herself able now to do, and that when the time came for intercession she would know it. "We must always thus, in our own efforts, strive to reach what we have not got, by the faithful practice of what we have."[13]

While it is right that we should not dally with intercession, we should know that, if we persist in it, we shall not escape some initiation into the cost of the redemptive process. We should not, on this account, pass it over or leave it out indefinitely from our prayers. By means of it, we may come, more swiftly than at almost any other point, into a really living relationship with others. "It is only in prayer that we can communicate with one another at the deepest level of our being," writes Bede Griffiths in his autobiography, *The Golden String*. "Behind all words and gestures, behind all thoughts and feelings, there is an inner centre of prayer where we can meet one another in the presence of God."[14]

For many persons it is a fact that they can pray for others at times when they cannot pray for themselves. Charles Péguy has put into his great poem, *The Mystery of the Charity of Joan of Arc,* a passionate cry of horror at the thought of being saved alone: There is a sense, he says, in which we save ourselves together. We arrive together at the place where the Lord is found. We should not go looking for the good Lord without the others. "We must all go back together to our father's house."[15]

Intercession also may be made for the unraveling of situations, for the resolution of destructive relations between nations or groups or institutions, or for the purification of corporate life. A saintly German poet-historian, the late Reinhold Schneider, told me shortly after the Second World War that the cynical attitude of the world toward acts of generosity and purity reminded him of the situation on the moon, where, because no atmosphere is present, no living thing could exist. "We must restore to the earth a spiritual atmosphere so that deeds of greatness and nobility can breathe here again, and we can only create this by the passionate practice of intercessory prayer." Down through the ages, individuals and groups have not failed to recreate such an atmosphere and by this means have again and again purified our corporate life from within.

PRAYER *and* SPIRITUAL HEALING

Finally, what of intercessory prayer for the healing of disease? In principle, this has already been dealt with in rejecting any final line that can be drawn between the psychical and the physical. Psychosomatic medicine today would have no quarrel about the effectiveness of prayer and its therapeutic effects in helping to prevent disease in the person who prays. Doctors may conclude that prayer for another person suffering from disease might have a beneficial effect if the sufferer knew that others cared enough for him or her to pray. In this case the knowledge of the existence of these prayers might help to restore the patient's own faith in an ultimate restoration to health.

But suppose the person who is ill did not know of these prayers that were made for him or her. Is there a power in prayer that can act upon the life of another (through the Being of God in which they are both bottomed) and that could contribute directly to healing—even when the whole operation is carried out in secret?

There is a good deal of evidence to affirm the efficacy of such secret intercessory prayer. This means no more and no less than that intercessory prayer seems able to touch the life of another at the core of his or her being and that in the extremity of disease we can be supported and even healed by the help of the prayers of others of whom we outwardly know nothing. As poet Alfred, Lord Tennyson wrote, "More things are wrought by prayer than this world dreams of. . . ."[16]

Does this mean, then, that intercessory prayer should be kept a secret and that the person prayed for had better not know of its existence? That does not seem necessarily to be implied. Often the knowledge of others' caring enough to pray for us is an added factor in our recovery. Such knowledge is in itself most heartening to an ill person who feels isolated and forlorn and cut off from life. Often, too, such knowledge leads the person to search his or her own faith and to cooperate, by fresh efforts at prayer and faith, with the healing power of God so that the person knows that at the heart of things "all shall be well."

We can be quite sure that much mischief could be done by taking too seriously the theme of Lloyd Douglas's popular novel, *The Magnificent Obsession,* which almost makes a magical fetish out of hiding from others any attempts made to help them. Still, we must confess that there is a cleanness in secret intercessory prayer. It is spared the curse of many of the corruptions that come from publicizing prayer and its favorable result simply for publicity's sake. In secret intercessory prayer all of the glibness and "virtuousness" and sunny altruism of "I'll pray for you" is absent, and yet the costly engagement, the vigil of deep work for the life of the other, is fully present.

I have always sensed the power that must have been present in the pastoral intercessory prayers of Jean Frederic Oberlin in that Ban de la Roche parsonage in Alsace in the late-eighteenth century. That morning hour between nine and ten—when the parishioners are reported to have tiptoed by and talked in hushed voices as they passed the parsonage, knowing that the pastor was praying for them—seems to me almost a model of true pastoral power in the community.

Yet I think I am still more moved by an incident Oberlin reported only long after it happened. He had ridden horseback all night in returning from one of his begging missions in Strasbourg. On reaching Ban de la Roche, at the break of day, he got off his horse at the crest of the hill overlooking the town and, falling on his knees, he poured out his heart to God for the spiritual and material needs of that miserably poor and backward community. This he did without anyone but himself and God knowing what was going on. The last word on secret versus nonsecret intercessory prayer is simply this: that each has its place.

CHAPTER FOUR

THE DIALOGUE
of
PRAYER *and* ACTION

The gist of the post-resurrection message of Jesus to his disciples has been summed up in the words, "Peace! I am alive. There is work for you to do." This message points not only to the ground of intercessory prayer but to the reenlistment into the labor force of the kingdom of God the full resources of the one who prays. Indeed there is work for you to do, and real prayer seldom concludes without some intimation of a work assignment. For if prayer in one sense is a disengagement—a stepping aside from life in order to look at it in the deepest perspective, to see it under the gaze of God—it does not stop there.

Contemplation is not a state of coma or of religious reverie. If it is genuine prayer, we find our inward life quickened. We sense new directions, or our attention is refocused on neglected ones. We find ourselves being mobilized and our inward resources regrouped in response to the new assignment. We find, in short, that we have been reenlisted in the redemptive order, that, in these ranks, our former reservations are brushed to one side and a new level of expendability emerges.

There is no denying the presence of our reservations. There is in each of us a set of invisible lines, of claimful preferences, and of self-chosen priorities for which the furnace of prayer is a refining fire. A couple asked for guidance in finding a property where they could carry out a piece of religious and humanitarian work, and were taken aback when a prompt prospect appeared that might transfer them to a strange and distant part of the country. Their request for guidance had had its geographical priorities! In 1784, a Quaker wife of a New Jersey printer reported piously to the Meeting of Burlington, New Jersey, that she was weighing the possibility of returning to Britain. "I am quite resigned to go or stay," she said. "But I am more resigned to go!"

The late Howard Thurman, one of the most revered African-American religious leaders in this country, once told me of an incident that took place in his Fellowship Church in San Francisco where African Americans, whites, and Asian Americans all worshiped together. A woman from the congregation asked him to call on her, and when he came, she proceeded to outline to him seven reasons why she could never join the Fellowship Church. The seventh reason was that she simply could not stand African Americans! Howard

Thurman laughed and told her he hoped that none of these reasons would keep her from continuing at least to attend the church, and he added that none of us could ever be quite sure what God might do with our objections. Now and then over the course of the next months, this woman appeared in the line of those who spoke to him after the service. She offered cryptic reports that "Number one is gone," or "Five has disappeared," but always with the addition, "Seven is still there." Finally one Sunday she came to him and said, "Oh, Dr. Thurman, even seven is gone, and I want to join the church." In real prayer, our most staunchly preferred reservations, guidances, and point-sevens are brushed quietly aside as we are reengaged and drawn into the work of the kingdom.

THE SEEDS *of* CONCERN

In prayer, the seeds of concern have a way of appearing. Often enough, a concern begins in a feeling of being personally liable and responsible for someone or some event. With it there may come an intimation that one should do some little thing: speak to some person, make an inquiry into a certain situation, write a letter, send some money, send a book. Or it may be a "stop" in our minds about some pending decision, or a clear directive that now is not the time to rest, or an urge to stay home when we had been meaning to be away. It may be that no more than this will be given us. But this seed is given us to follow, and if we do not follow it, we cannot expect to see what may grow from it. Seeds, not fruit, are given in prayer, but they are given for planting. "It is hardly ever possible to see from the start all that God is to mean to one," writes Adrienne von Speyr. "Once open to the light, [we] may ask God to claim [us] more essentially and more profoundly. But on one condition only, on condition that [we do] not refuse the first small act that God demands of [us]."[1]

A young physician once hung out a sign, "Small fevers gratefully accepted," and in prayer there must be no less willingness to be open for the small nudges, the gentle pressures, the delicate tugs on the sleeve. Emma Noble, upon an occasion of worship in England, felt drawn to go to visit the most depressed coal miners in the Rhondda Valley in South Wales. When she got there, it was clear to her that those on the side of the valley she had gone to visit were not open to any assistance that she or the Society of Friends could give to them. She did not feel easy about returning home, however, so she went to the other side of the valley. There opportunities began to open and the purpose of her journey began slowly to emerge. Out of this concern, a long-term program of work unfolded that involved university people, members of Parliament, a royal visit, and eventually a program of legislation to alter the ugly situation. If she had not taken the first step, which was in part a mistaken one, the rest could hardly have taken place as it did.

Victor Gollancz, speaking at a peace meeting in London, cited an old Hebrew legend that declared when Moses struck the Red Sea with his stick, nothing happened. It was only when the first man plunged in that the sea opened. There is a classic remark of Luther's: "Had Moses waited until he understood how Israel could elude Pharaoh's armies, they might have been in Egypt still." Prayer demands that we act, and that—having acted in accordance with our leading in prayer—we bear the consequences of our acts, even when we cannot foresee all that they are to cost.

There is a further feature of the following out of these concerns that rise in prayer. There is a sense in which the power of prayer indwells them even when they have passed from intention into action. It is not alone as in a truly personal act where it can be said that its goodness comes from the act's being all of one piece: what I am is what I do. Now it is not only what I am, but it is also what God is that threads into this act and gives it the power to open the life around it. It is this which makes it more than a sundered, separate event, that in fact makes it rather a part of a living current that the prayer and the faithfulness in following out the prayer have unleashed in the situation.

CONCERNS *and* RATIONAL SCRUTINY

There is in all of this no claim for infallibility. We do not deny that we may be mistaken in the way we have chosen to follow out the leadings of prayer. Certainly these leadings come to us by the route of our own psychological mechanisms and are capable, therefore, of being distorted. But those who live in this kind of abandonment and who have tuned their ears to "listen to the pulses of the divine whisper" are almost debonair about being mistaken, even about being made a fool of. They know there is always further prayer—and in it is a source of correction.

If the matter is one that might involve a considerable change of circumstances for themselves and their families, those who pray do not fear submitting it to the customary rational scrutinies. How does the concern look in the cool light of the next day, of the next week? How does it look after we have unleashed our own private detective agency upon it and examined it from all of the searching angles that this bureau is capable of unearthing? How does it look after wise and trusted people have given their opinion of it? If the matter can endure this kind of treatment and suffer no more than a reshaping of its details, then it is to be carried out. If, however, the concern is neglected and allowed to fester within us, it seems to cut us off from future light.

As has already been said, no battery of tests can ever guarantee that a concern that comes in prayer may not be a mistaken one. Yet, if we are willing to have it questioned and are able to keep our faith in the living network into which our lives have been drawn, then if we take the wrong fork at any point, and its wrongness becomes clear, perhaps painfully clear to us, there is always the next fork of the road where we may be drawn back into the right direction.

It is somewhat comforting to see John Woolman, whose whole life was gathered up in trying to follow the Inward Guide, confess in his *Journal* the wakeful night he spent on his dangerous journey to Wehaloosing. He was tossing in troubled rescrutiny of his undertaking, while his companion slept quietly beside him. He feared that possibly he was continuing on the journey, not because God was drawing him, but rather because to turn back at this point would subject him to derision at home and the charge of cowardice. In short, the personal detective agency of even this spiritual veteran bluntly queried the validity of his concern when the outgoing journey was nearly completed. The *Journal* tells us that, after a night's inward review of the situation, the agency's query was rejected, and his mind set at ease, "and I got a little sleep towards morning."[2]

At times this inner direction of prayer not only lays on us a new sense of liability or responsibility for another person, but opens our eyes afresh to what in God's hands this life

might become. The tiny wild gladiolas of the Angola veldt—
that break into blossom at the end of the Central African
winter—require a pair of illumined eyes to connect them
with the majestic floral spikes that they have become under
cultivation in the West. Prayer supplies such illumined eyes
and makes us able to see in another person one destined for
a vocation under God. If we are favored in communicating
this insight to the other person, we may become an instrument in arousing that vocation in him or her. Von Hügel, in
his prayers for the gifted literary historian of religion Evelyn
Underhill, early discerned a woman marked out for sanctity
and for being a spiritual guide to her generation. His faithfulness in directing her was not in vain, for before his death
he kindled in her an awareness of this very calling.

FOREIGN *and* DOMESTIC MUTATIONS

Prayer may lead to astonishing mutations or changes. It may
spur new developments, such as the original Franciscan
Third Order. In the sixteenth century the Swedish archbishop Laurentius Petri accepted the king's offer of a bodyguard on condition that he might recruit it from poor and
deserving students whom he sent to Uppsala for religious
studies on the king's payroll. A prospering physician in mid-
career was drawn to leave a well-doctored Texas city and to
go with his family to a mid-African mission station until

further notice. A British woman missionary to Uganda, shelved by tuberculosis, followed the inward leading and set up what eventually became St. Julian's House[3]—a furlough and inspirational rest center where missionaries could shed their physical, mental, and spiritual numbness and be prepared for the next stage of work to which they were called.

Do these instances seem formidable and remote? Quite as often, prayer calls for domestic mutations: not for leaving home or post or present companions, but for living differently among them. The Muslim writer Hallaj describes how a Muslim, when he cannot go on the coveted pilgrimage to Mecca, may construct in his own yard a simple square enclosure where, on the day of pilgrimage, he can make the circuit and perform the ceremonies as he would have done at Mecca. In addition, the instructions read, "Let him gather together thirty orphans for whom he has prepared the most exquisite feast he can get; let him bring them to his home and serve them that feast; and, after waiting on them himself and washing their hands as a servant himself, let him present each of them with a new frock, and give them each seven dirhams. This will be a substitute for Pilgrimage."[4] How often prayer provides us with a similar substitution for a pilgrimage.

Author Rufus Moseley once told of an able pastor who came to him and told him that he was going to resign. He said his people needed a better pastor than he was, a pastor with a deeper life of prayer and dedication. Moseley agreed about the congregation's need, but went on quietly to ask him why he was running away: "Instead, why do you not remain and with God's help become that better pastor?"

Prayer has sent men and women back into a difficult family situation, back to a school, back to an office, even back into their own careers, not to continue as before, but as under new management.

"A MAN *on the* CROSS SENDS ME BACK AGAIN"

In 1957 Pastor Hamel in Eastern Germany pointed out that many of his East German fellow Christians had remained in the Eastern section of Germany with their bodies, but in their minds and expectations they had already immigrated to the West. They were just marking time, waiting for the West to take over, hoping that if life got too hard, they could still go out to the West through Berlin. He called this "inward immigration" and warned them that they would never have the power of a Christian witness to their Communist brothers and sisters until they accepted the place where they were as the one in which they meant to live and die. They must be willing to trust themselves to God, and to live each day, not elsewhere, but precisely where they were.[5] Prayer often speaks with an almost identical admonition: The

Christian witness to be made not "then" but "now," not "there" but "here."

When in our human condition we grow impatient and are tempted to throw in the sponge, or at least to force the pace, the one who prays is likely to be recalled to commitment. In a critical situation Teresa of Ávila reported that she was inwardly instructed, "Now stand firm." A Japanese student with only a labored command of the English language once introduced himself to a group at Haverford College with the deliberately articulated sentence, "When listen to me, kindly expect slow motion." Slow motion, of course, affects even those who pray regularly, but it does not as often result in their throwing in the sponge. For again and again when the one who prays falters and is tempted to desert, there comes in prayer what George Tyrrell refers to as "a man on the cross [who] sends me back again."

This rugged persistence on the part of the one who prays is often charged off to habit and stolidity by those who do not understand its source and who do not grasp the basis of the confidence that is concealed there. During the long years of the Civil War, America's oldest college, William and Mary, was closed. Many accepted its future as doomed. An old custodian refused to accept this verdict, however. Each day for five years he rang the bells of this ghost college as though it still lived. At the end of five years, he rang them for a reopening that vindicated his vigil of faith.

The one who prays is made able to bear slow motion, the pace of the hen. That person is given a dogged persistence, grounded in an assurance that he or she does not work alone. Such pray-ers do not, to be sure, know precisely how Israel is to elude Pharaoh's armies, but they know that they have not been released and therefore they must carry on. This staying power, as worldly adversaries often discover, makes formidable opponents.

CHRISTIAN PRAYER *and* ETHICAL INTENSIFICATION

There is an ethical sharpening that takes place in real Christian prayer that is highly dangerous to any complacency concerning the order of things as they are. The life of Jesus Christ witnessed to God's infinite caring for the very hairs of our heads, and for the lost sheep. It is no accident, therefore, that in prayer, in the presence of Jesus Christ, we are brought inwardly before the revolutionary leveling of God's infinite concern for every soul that comes into the world. "Christianity taught us to care. Caring is the greatest thing—caring matters most."[6] These words of Baron von Hügel's are borne out in Christian prayer; for to come into the field of force of God's infinite caring is to feel inwardly the terrible pull of the unlimited liability for one another that the New Testament ethic lays upon us. This lays the knife at the root of every claim for special privilege and of all "comfortism," and no amount of theological casuistry can justify our disregarding it.

Medieval English writer Walter Hilton's dis-ease at our public efforts "to adorn Christ's brow but to leave His feet unattended" was not an exclusively fourteenth-century affliction. In our own time, we know all too well what philosopher Nikolay Berdyaev meant when he declared, "Bread for myself is an economic problem. Bread for my brother is a spiritual problem." "Bread" may mean anything from medical care and proper housing to our loving care of the aged and the insane. It may be concern for the social delinquents and their consignment to life as virtual outcasts from the living community. Sometimes, like a flash of lightning piercing the darkness and showing us the outlines of our situation with a terrible clarity, Christian prayer discloses to us the hard curd of corporate sin in our time: war, poverty, disease; and the shallow and loveless human relationships that blight friendships, family, community, and vocational situations. Prayer also reveals to us the flight into excessive extroversion that plagues our "technicized" West.

Christian prayer brings a relentless clarity. But underneath its fierce realism and its costly baptism of personal responsibility lays an equally steadying sense that in whatever we are called to do, we do not work alone, and that in spite of the lump of sin that is all too apparent, there is a great legacy of goodness to be drawn upon in humankind. Chain reactions of goodness may be released that carry im- measurable power. We must never lose faith in this fact. Again the triple "All shall be well, and all shall be well, and all manner of thing shall be well" undergirds the specific acts of well-doing that are called for in prayer. It is because of this assurance that one often notes in those who pray, even in the midst of overwhelming odds, what journalist G. K. Chesterton called an "asceticism of cheerfulness in contrast to the easier asceticism of melancholy." It is as though the one who prays were called upon to live as a fourth dimen- sionalist in a traditionally three-dimensional world.

WHAT *of* PRAYER *without* CEASING?

There are still some troublesome questions about prayer that we must face before concluding. What of those like Brother Lawrence,[7] and Thomas Kelly,[8] and Frank Laubach[9] who urge perpetual prayer and speak of the New Testament in- junction to "pray without ceasing" (1 Thessalonians 5:17, KJV)? What do they mean? How can I pray when I am con- centrating upon my other duties? Is this not impossible? Does God, who has created us and put us in the exacting work of this world, require our exclusive attention?

These legitimate queries, I believe, can be answered with- out contradicting what Paul, Brother Lawrence, Kelly, and

Laubach commend. For there is a true sense in which—when we love greatly—this love goes on back of all else that we do. Far from blocking our creative efforts on the immediate tasks before us, this undergirding love may heighten our powers for all that we do. If we love God, if we acknowledge joyfully to whom we belong, if, in the intervals between our other tasks, this love moves naturally to the surface and gives a glow to all that we do, this *is* prayer without ceasing, perpetual prayer.

Of course we give full attention to the task before us. We need not rattle off the Lord's Prayer while designing a pattern for a new tool or fitting a new dress. In perpetual prayer, there is something that frames all that we do, something that goes on day and night beneath the stream of our consciousness: a gratitude, an adoration, an acknowledgment of creatureliness—of dependence upon God, that we are God's and God made us—a sense of encompassment. If it is suggested that in order to be truly a Christian, the unconscious life must be involved, it is here that the advocates of ceaseless prayer are on incontrovertible ground. Often "prayer without ceasing" is connected with swift, ejaculatory prayers such as, "Keep a firm hold on me, O Lord" or "My God, my all" that we flash into the midst of our busy occupations, when the clock strikes, or when we change from one occupation to another. But these quick prayers are only contributory to the deep, abiding, undergirding reaching out for God that our exponents of perpetual prayer advocate.

PRAYER *and the* "NIGHT SHIFTS"

Another area in the life of prayer inevitably comes up for questioning. What shall we do about the "dry times," the seasons when all the desire for prayer has left us and when prayer is the last thing in which we feel we want to engage? Isn't it wrong to force ourselves to pray? Shouldn't real prayer be so attractive that we would hurry to get into the place of prayer, run to get there? What if, instead, we feel the greatest resistance to praying at all? Is this not a sign to stop and take a vacation from prayer until the desire returns?

Obviously, if we are suffering from some physical or mental illness that has heavily sapped our vitality, this needs attention and should get it. But the feeling of dryness in prayer is so common and so universal that it must not be permitted to make us run for cover and hide behind some physical ailment. There are too many occasions when prayer is deeply distasteful to us, although the mind and body were never sounder. Should I give it up? The answer is an unequivocal *No.*

All prayer reaches plateaus where it loses the initial exhil-

aration of climbing. These are the times when a consolida-
tion of our commitment may be taking place. In such times
the testing of our real loyalty is in process. Anyone can pray
when the heart is bubbling over; no loyalty is needed then.
But when the spirit is dry and all surface desire gone, then is
the time when we learn to whom we really belong. No one
has expressed this better than François de Sales who insisted
that when we cannot give God fresh roses, we give him dry
ones for "the dry have more strength and sweetness."[10]

It should be clear to us that we are in this business for the
long pull, for fair weather and foul, through sickness and
health, and that it is perfectly natural that we should run
into these rough patches, these "night shifts," these dark
nights, and that then, as never before, our prayers are
needed.

We should do well at this point, as in the case of persistent distractions, to examine ourselves as to whether some
unfaced decision, some unyielded barrier, some personal relationship that needs correction stands back of this blackout
in our desire for prayer. Closely linked to this must be our
realization that—if we are really touching the stream of divine causality in our prayers, and are sensing what major
changes in us are called for in order to continue in this
stream—it is almost inevitable that our own inner strategist
will seek to hinder this change. And how could this be done

more readily than by causing a distaste for prayer and luring us toward a hundred counter calls?

It is here that our faithfulness will tell who it is we mean to serve. Only the sentimentalists depict prayer as a perpetual April. A good deal of prayer is framed in fall and winter, and much of the real work of prayer is best done in these very seasons. Does a painter stop painting when the exhilaration palls? Does a writer lay aside her book on which she is working if she is not in a glow of creativity? An Indian man of prayer notes, "In spite of monsoon or summer heat, the Ganges never stops, so why should I?" A line in the Book of Ecclesiastes says, "He who observes the wind will not sow; and he who regards the clouds will not reap. . . . In the morning, sow your seed" (Ecclesiastes 11:4,6). This speaks the right word for dealing with times of dryness in prayer.

PRIVATE PRAYER *and* CORPORATE WORSHIP

What of the relationship of prayer to corporate worship? Does the following have about it a familiar ring? "I have come to be able to find God in prayer and perhaps in a small prayer group, but the corporate worship of the church palls on me, and although I am hesitant to admit it openly, I feel that I could get on perfectly well without the public worship." It must be freely admitted that this feeling may come to nearly all persons at some stage in their life of prayer.

This scruple has a certain validity to it, in that the person who has found a living, firsthand contact with God in prayer is holding this norm up to the church and demanding that its corporate services of worship should accomplish regularly for its members the same transforming awareness of God's abiding presence. But the scruple has also its dark side, namely, a certain puffed-up spirit of loftiness, of pride, of superiority that goes badly with the fellowship in Christ into which the one who prays is called. For all of its faults and frailties, the institutional church, year after year, does with great steadiness confront men and women with the witness to God and to what God did, does, and would do for men and women in our world.

It is well for us to recall that the Christian witness and the Christian task of saving the world were borne to us by the church and that, in its service, more than a hundred generations of men and women of every race, nationality, and psychological type have made their responses to Jesus Christ and to his revelation of God's incredible love and mercy. When we come to a service of worship, we should come to participate, to bring our praise and honor and thanks—as well as our needs—and lay them at God's feet in the midst of this great mixed community of the present and the past. In this act, we are lifted out of our private world into a public one, out of our personal situations into a social situation. We join with the fellowship, both openly and outwardly, as well as in our private life of prayer. The humbling, enlarging, encompassing fellowship into which the church's corporate exercise sweeps us is a part of the Christian experience that we dare not forgo if we are able to attend. Those who live in remote places, or who by illness are deprived of this regular experience, witness to the impoverishment they suffer.

The church also renders to us a service by its anchor-like reminding both of God's gift and of the demands God makes upon us and the society in which we live. The church rekindles our quenched spirits when they are dry and torpid; it expands our horizons, making us aware of the neglected dimensions of the Christian life still absent from our awareness. The church not only renders these services, but it has a right to expect us to contribute to its common life, to reach out to others through its offices, to be present at its services, and to offer our continual prayers that it may be the Holy Spirit's living instrument in the world, for which it was called into being.

The query may continue, "Is not belief in the church inherited, and is not my attendance there merely a habit for a good deal of the time?" The answer would certainly need to be a wholehearted agreement that church attendance is most assuredly a vast habit. It is both a good habit and a divinely appointed habit, and one that we are entrusted with preserving and improving.

In this connection it might be recalled that a consistent life of prayer is also a habit, and the sooner we can mobilize our mental and spiritual forces and establish a degree of regularity in its practice, the better. Pascal in his *Thoughts* has some stern words for religious sentimentalists. After noting that we "are [people] and not angels," he goes on to suggest that we should not overlook the fact that we are "as much automatic as intellectual."[11] Our task is to assemble our human resources (instinctive, automatic impulses) around those things that can center them on what is highest (Philippians 4:8), instead of permitting them to be enlisted for a lifetime of slavery to that which debases and animalizes.

We might conclude with Evelyn Underhill's delicious words to one who was a little too fastidious to be content with the existing church or its clergy. In her *Letters,* Evelyn Underhill writes, "The Church is an 'essential service' like the Post Office, but there will always be some narrow, irritating and inadequate officials behind the counter and you will always be tempted to exasperation by them."[12] But "I feel the regular, steady, docile practice of corporate worship is of the utmost importance for the building-up of your spiritual life. . . . No amount of solitary reading [or prayer] makes up for humble immersion in the life and worship of the

Church. . . . The corporate and personal together make up the Christian ideal."[13] As for private prayer versus corporate worship: Continue the one; do not neglect the other. Little needs to be added on this issue.

"LENT to BE SPENT"

Always in authentic Christian prayer, self-giving increases. The realization that one is personally expendable for the work of the kingdom grows. We find in it a companionship and a sense of having found at last that for which we were born, that which lifts us up when we relapse. Arthur Gossip tells of visiting members in his Glasgow, Scotland, parish and coming late in the afternoon, tired and inwardly exhausted, to the doorway of a five-story tenement where a parishioner of his lived on the top floor. He stopped and said to himself, "I've had enough. I'll come tomorrow." Then he said he seemed to feel a presence brush past him and to see dimly a pair of stooped gray shoulders start up the stairs with the words, "Then I shall have to go alone." Gossip said this was enough to draw him over the threshold, and they went together.

The final dimension in Christian prayer is this readiness to be used, the knowledge that life is "lent to be spent." The one who really prays knows by firsthand experience what medieval spiritual writer Jan Van Ruysbroeck meant when he said, "The love of Jesus is both avid and generous. All that He is and all that He has, He gives. All that we are and all that we have, He takes."

NOTES

Introduction

1. Charles Williams, *All Hallows Eve* (London: Faber, 1945).
2. George Bernanos, *The Diary of a Country Priest*, trans. by Pamela Morris (New York: The Macmillan Co., 1948), p. 163.
3. Søren Kierkegaard, *Point of View* (New York: Oxford University Press, 1939), p. 43.
4. From *The Complete Works of Saint Teresa*, Volume II, trans. and ed. by E. Allison Peers from the critical edition of P. Silverio de Santa Teresa, C.D., published by Sheed & Ward, Inc., New York.
5. Teresa of Jesus [Ávila], *The Way of Perfection*, revised by F. B. Zimmerman (London: Baker, 1919), p. 27.
6. P. T. Forsyth, *The Soul of Prayer* (London: Independent Press, Ltd., 1954), pp. 68–69.
7. Marius Grout, "On Contemplation," trans. by Blanche Shaffer, in *Friends World News*, Birmingham, England, No. 16, 1945, p. 1.
8. Ibid.

1. Prayer and the Human Situation

1. Saint Augustine, *Confessions*, trans. by Henry Chadwick (Oxford, Engl.: Oxford University, 1991), pp. 183–84.
2. Blaise Pascal, *Pensées [Thoughts]* (New York: Random House, The Modern Library, 1941), No. 552, p. 176.
3. Abbé de Tourville, *Letters of Direction* (London: Dacre Press, 1939), p. 72.
4. Friedrich von Hügel, *Selected Letters* (London: Dent, 1927), p. 62.
5. Dietrich Bonhoeffer, *Letters and Papers from Prison* (New York: Macmillan, 1953), pp. 165–66, 191.
6. Thomas Traherne, *Centuries* (New York: Harper & Bros., 1960), pp. 3–4.
7. George Fox, *Journal* (New York: E. P. Dutton, 1940), p. 11.

8. Dame Juliana of Norwich, *Revelations*, ed. by G. Barrack (London: Methuen, 1901), Chap. XXVII, p. 56.
9. *Journal of John Wesley*, ed. by Nehemiah Curnock, Standard Edition (New York: Eaton & Mains, 1909–1916).
10. *The Prayers of Kierkegaard*, ed. by Perry D. LeFèvre (Chicago: University of Chicago, 1956), p. 202.
11. Paul Claudel, *Letters to a Doubter* (London: Burns, Oates and Washbourne, Ltd., 1927), p. 24.
12. Umphrey Lee, *John Wesley and Modern Religion* (Nashville: Cokesbury, 1936), pp. 107–108.
13. Teresa of Jesus [Ávila], *The Way of Perfection*, pp. 153, 97.
14. Gerhard Tersteegen, *The Quiet Way* (London: Epworth Press, 1950), p. 15.
15. Friedrich von Hügel, *Selected Letters*, p. 64.
16. Teresa of Jesus [Ávila], *The Way of Perfection*, p. 176.
17. Ibid., p. 145.
18. Simone Weil, *Waiting on God* (London: Routledge & Kegan Paul, 1951), pp. 23–24.
19. Rueben P. Job and Norman Shawchuck, *A Guide to Prayer for All God's People* (Nashville: Upper Room Books, 1990).
20. *The Book of Common Prayer* (New York: The Church Hymnal Corporation and The Seabury Press, 1977).
21. Lancelot Andrewes, *The Private Devotions of Lancelot Andrewes* (Nashville: Abingdon Press, 1950).
22. Teresa of Jesus [Ávila], *The Way of Perfection*, p. 144.

2. To Pray Is to Change

1. E. Herman, *Creative Prayer* (New York: Harper & Bros., 1934).
2. Russell Maltby, *Obiter Scripta* (London: Epworth, 1952), p. 91.
3. Søren Kierkegaard, *Journals* (New York: Oxford University, 1938), pp. 472, 484.
4. Blaise Pascal, *Pensées [Thoughts]*, No. 139, p. 48.
5. *Journal of George Fox*, Everyman edition (New York: E. P. Dutton, 1948), p. 35.

6. Teresa of Jesus [Ávila], *The Way of Perfection*, p. 95.
7. Russell Maltby, *Obiter Scripta*, p. 98.
8. Olive Wyon, *On the Way* (Philadelphia: Westminster, 1958).
9. Teresa of Jesus [Ávila], *The Way of Perfection*, p. 62.
10. C. S. Lewis, *The Screwtape Letters* (New York: Macmillan, 1943).
11. Thomas E. Powers, *First Questions in the Life of the Spirit* (New York: Harper & Bros., 1959), pp. 148–49.

3. The Power of Prayer

1. P. T. Forsyth, *The Soul of Prayer*, p. 66.
2. Teresa of Jesus [Ávila], *The Interior Castle*, p. 107.
3. P. T. Forsyth, *The Soul of Prayer*, p. 80.
4. Hermann Hagerdorn, "Prayer during Battle," in *A Treasury of Poems for Worship and Devotion*, ed. by Charles L. Wallis (New York: Harper & Bros., 1959), p. 207.
5. Cyril Powell, *Secrets of Answered Prayer* (New York: Thos. Y. Crowell, 1960), p. 68.
6. Douglas V. Steere, *Prayer and Worship* (New York: Association Press, 1938), pp. 29–30.
7. Friedrich von Hügel, *Selected Letters*, p. 269.
8. Charles Williams, *Descent into Hell* (London: Faber, 1949).
9. Blaise Pascal, *Pensées [Thoughts]*, No. 513, p. 140.
10. P. T. Forsyth, *The Soul of Prayer*, p. 45.
11. Alexander Whyte, *Thomas Shepard, Pilgrim Father and Founder of Harvard*, quoted in *A Diary of Readings*, comp. by John Baillie (New York: Chas. Scribner's Sons, 1955), Day 273.
12. Margaret Cropper, *The Life of Evelyn Underhill* (New York: Harper & Bros., 1958), p. 107.
13. Ibid.
14. Bede Griffiths, *The Golden String* (New York: P. J. Kennedy & Sons, 1955), p. 130.
15. Charles Péguy, *The Mystery of the Charity of Joan of Arc*, Julian Green, trans. (New York: Pantheon, Inc., 1950), p. 39.
16. Alfred, Lord Tennyson, "Morte D'Arthur," line 415.

4. The Dialogue of Prayer and Action

1. Adrienne von Speyr, *The Word,* trans. by Alexander Dru (London: Collins, 1953), p. 9.

2. John Woolman, *Journal* (New York: Houghton-Mifflin, 1871), pp. 196–97. Also see Douglas V. Steere, *Doors into Life* (New York: Harper & Bros., 1948), p. 109.

3. J. H. Oldham, *Florence Allshorn* (New York: Harper & Bros., 1950).

4. Eric Schroeder, *Muhammad's People* (Portland, M.E.: Bond, Wheelright, 1955), p. 548.

5. Johannes Hamel, *A Christian in East Germany,* trans. by Ruth and Charles West (New York: Association Press, 1960), chapter 1.

6. *Letters from Baron Friedrich von Hügel to a Niece,* ed. by Gwendolen Greene (New York: E. P. Dutton & Co., 1928), p. xliii.

7. Brother Lawrence, *The Practice of the Presence of God* (Westwood, N.J.: Fleming H. Revell, 1958).

8. Thomas Kelly, *A Testament of Devotion* (New York: Harper & Bros., 1941).

9. Frank C. Laubach, *Letters of a Modern Mystic* (Westwood, N.J.: Fleming H. Revell, 1937).

10. François de Sales, *Introduction to the Devout Life,* trans. by J. K. Ryan (New York: Doubleday, 1960), p. 260.

11. Blaise Pascal, *Pensées [Thoughts],* No. 140, p. 53; No. 358, p. 118; No. 252, p. 89.

12. *Letters of Evelyn Underhill* (New York: Longmans, Green, 1947), p. 208.

13. Ibid., p. 261.